INSIGHT POCKET GUIDES

Seychelles

GW00602711

APA PUBLICATIONS

Part of the Langenscheidt Publishing Group

L

Welcome!

The Seychelles' 115 islands were created many millennia ago when India broke away from Africa, somewhere close to Madagascar, and drifted across the Indian Ocean, leaving the granite fragments of the Seychelles in its wake.

In these pages Insight's specialists on the Seychelles, Judith and Adrian Skerrett, have designed a series of itineraries to help you get the most out of the islands during a short stay. Mahé and Praslin are the obvious hubs for your exploration: full-day orientation drives through these islands reveal their secrets. Then, using the Pick and Mix selections, you could opt for a morning tour of the capital, an afternoon exploring a shady coco de mer forest, or a whole day chasing a sailfish, snorkelling or discovering the tranquillity of an uninhabited island. There are giant tortoises and rare birds to find, ox carts to ride and fresh fish to barbecue. The Excursions section suggests overnight stays at the coral islands of Bird and Desroches, perfect for getting away from it all. If you've come specifically to cruise, sail, dive, fish or hike, a separate Activities section covers all these possibilities. Supporting these sections are chapters on history and culture, eating out, nightlife and practical information, including advice on hotels.

Judith and Adrian Skerrett first washed up on the Seychelles' pristine shores in 1980, intending to work for just two years. Many years later, however, they are still here. Keen naturalists and authors of several guides on the Seychelles, the Skerrets love the stunning natural beauty of their adopted home, describing some of the idyllic islands as 'the stuff of dreams'.

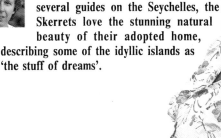

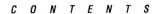
C O N T E N T S

*Pages 2/3:
dream seene,
Anse Lazio
beach on
Praslin*

Excursions

Pages 8/9: the fairy tern is an emblem of Seychelles' national airline

Activities

Shopping, Eating Out & Nightlife

Calendar of Events

Practical Information

Maps

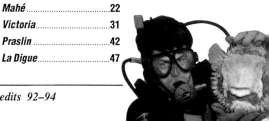

HISTORY

W hat makes the Seychelles is-
lands the way they are is their splendid isolation. Literally a thousand miles from anywhere – India to the north, Africa to the west,
Sri Lanka to the east and Madagascar to the south – they were uninhabited until the late 18th century. Thus, while the natural
beauty of other Indian Ocean islands was gradually decimated, that
of the Seychelles has been preserved.

Early Contact

The first people to have contact with the Seychelles may have been
Arab traders in the 9th century. There is no evidence for this as yet,
but it seems unlikely that these great voyagers did not stumble upon
Seychelles. When Portuguese explorer Vasco da Gama sailed across
this ocean, he had an Arab pilot on board with him. The Portuguese may have learnt of Seychelles from such Arab geographers,
though there is no record of the latter visiting the granitic islands.

In 1501, another famous Portuguese explorer, Jean de Nova gave
his name to an island in the coralline group (now Farquhar), and
in 1505, da Gama sailed through and named the Amirantes
islands, but no attempt was made to colonise them.

The British, who were next on the scene, showed a
similar disinterest. A merchant vessel, the *Ascension*
arrived off Mahé in January 1609. The islands appeared uninhabited to the crew. They reported an excellent harbour and that good supplies were available,
but no one back home took the bait.

Piracy

From 1690 to 1720, many pirates were based in
Madagascar. The new flow of merchant shipping in
the Indian Ocean made these vessels easy prey for
them. Seychelles' isolation made it an ideal hideout
and it seems likely that the pirates took advantage
of this to make repairs and store supplies.

Although there is no direct proof that pirates

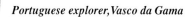

Portuguese explorer, Vasco da Gama

A wall on Frégate reputedly built by pirates

visited Seychelles, rumours of buried treasure abound on the islands. The most famous legend is that of Le Vasseur – recounted in the *Mahé Day 1 Itinerary* – but since the earliest settlement of the islands, there have been other tales. Many Seychellois are convinced that certain local families founded their fortunes on caches they had unearthed. On Fregate, you may come across ruins associated with pirates: in 1911, some silver coins, forks, spoons, shoebuckles and a bosun's whistle were found on Astove, an island in the Aldabra group.

However, the pirates' heyday in the region soon ended. Trading concerns with India were too important, and the English and French colonial powers sent their navies to police the area. At one time, as many as 17 pirate ships, with over 1,500 men had been active; but by 1719, a visitor to Madagascar could only find 17 men who said they were pirates – all of whom longed to go home. For every pirate who made it back to a prosperous retirement, there were a dozen who were killed in action, murdered by rivals, drank themselves to an early grave, or starved when money ran out. Life under the Jolly Roger was not all 'yo ho ho and a bottle of rum!'

A French Possession

Trading interests in the region had already motivated the French to occupy Bourbon (Reunion) in 1663, and the Île de France (Mauritius) in 1721. They found it worrying to have the Seychelles islands, which the British might occupy, in close proximity to their bases. At the time, the French had the Indian Ocean islands to themselves and they wanted no competition on their doorstep.

In 1742, Frenchman Captain Lazare Picault

The Stone of Possession laid by the French

was sent to report on the Seychelles. It was decided that they were of sufficient interest to merit a second voyage in 1744. This time, Picault brought back detailed charts, and named Mahé in honour of the governor of Mauritius. The name Seychelles was that of a French finance minister – Viscount Jean Moreau de Séchelles – given in 1756 when Captain Nicholas Morphey was sent to claim the islands for France.

As the governors of Mauritius were responsible for Seychelles, they had to ensure that the new colony did not cost too much. Therefore, the governors must have been pleased when Brayer du Barré, a private entrepreneur from France, undertook the settlement of Seychelles as a speculative venture. Du Barré was given little finance or support. He sent 26 colonists to Seychelles in August 1770, who landed on St Anne Island. Meanwhile, somewhat sneakily, the French government decided to establish their own settlement on Mahé where Pierre Poivre, the administrator of Mauritius, encouraged the growing of spices. Slaves were brought to do the hard work.

Bust of Pierre Poivre

After initial success, du Barré's settlement failed. It did not have enough support from the authorities, and du Barré bankrupted himself. His settlers started making money by selling tortoises and timber to passing ships rather than farming. Many moved to Mahé and set up camps in the hills above Victoria. The government settlement at Anse Royale struggled along. In the end, most of du Barré's people were evacuated, though one man, Gillot, soldiered on alone at Anse Royale until the colony was re-established in 1778.

The Days of de Quincy

Jean Baptiste Queau de Quincy guided the colony through difficult war years and lifted Seychelles out of the doldrums. The administrator arrived in 1793; soon after which England and France were at war. Quincy knew it would be pointless to resist: he capitulated, but only until the British warship sailed out of sight. In all, he made seven capitulations to the English captains, a move which did not require Seychelles to become British, and guaranteed security for the property of the Seychellois. Once the ships had left, Seychelles was neutral and French warships were made welcome.

In 1801, the arrival of 70 'terrorists' deported by Napoleon from France, following an attempt on his life, caused more problems for Quincy. Most had reputations for having carried out some of the worst outrages of the Revolution. However, very few stayed here. Some escaped but the majority were re-deported to the Comores.

Mauritius finally fell to the British and in 1812, Seychelles became a British colony. Quincy was kept on by the British to run Seychelles. He later became a Justice of the Peace and was a respected figure in the colony until his death in 1827.

There were early, but not very serious attempts to stamp out slave trading in Seychelles. An act of 1807 had made slave trading illegal in Britain and her colonies, although it was still possible to own slaves. Full emancipation finally came in 1839 and owners were paid compensation for the slaves they had lost.

Former slaves found it was easy to live in Seychelles without working, and understandably chose not to. The ex-owners found it hard to adjust to having to pay for workers. They felt farming was almost impossible without slaves and some chose to live off their compensation payments instead. Many emigrated; others decided to plant their estates with coconut palms, since it took less labour to produce coconuts than to grow the traditional cash crops of cotton, sugar and maize. Seychelles now had the typical social structure of an ex-French colony; rich planters, or the *gran blan*, usually of French origin, who enjoyed most of the wealth while those of African descent scraped a living from the sea, or small gardens where they grew vegetables. Those of mixed parentage, or the *blan koko* (the not so well-off whites), fell between the two levels.

Salvation for the economy came in the form of almost 3,000 'liberated Africans', rescued from Arab slave traders by British anti-slaving patrols on the east African coast between 1861 and 1874. They were a source of cheap labour for the plantations. Exports of coconut oil increased; vanilla also became a valuable cash crop. Seychelles prospered and the population grew steadily. In 1903, Seychelles ceased to be a dependency of Mauritius.

A National Archives list of African slaves

Then, an artificial substitute was found for vanilla, and the market price plummeted. In addition, the outbreak of World War I meant that ships could not call to collect cargoes of coconut oil. By 1918, poverty was widespread. Crime figures soared as desperate people turned to theft. New cash crops such as cinnamon oil, guano and copra were introduced and helped the colony to survive the grim war years.

Government House, Seychelles. UNE BONNE ANNÉE W. E. DAVIDSON December 1905.

GOVERNMENT HOUSE
SEYCHELLES.

A 1905 photograph of the Government House

The Age of Politics

World War II caused more distress in the colony, leading to the formation of Seychelles' first political grouping, the Association of Seychelles Taxpayers. Although its members were mostly well-to-do planters, they spoke up against the colonial power on behalf of the Seychellois. In 1964, there was a more general politicisation of the country when the Seychelles Democratic Party (SDP) and Seychelles Peoples United Party (SPUP) were created, led by James Mancham and France Albert Rene respectively. The SDP wished to retain Seychelles' close ties with Britain, whilst the SPUP, a socialist party, pushed for autonomy.

In 1967, universal adult suffrage was introduced for elections to the Legislative Council. In 1970, this council became a 15-member Legislative Assembly in which, after elections, the SDP had six seats and the SPUP five. James Mancham of the SDP was therefore made Chief Minister by the British Governor. In the 1974 elections, SDP won 52.4 percent of the votes and SPUP 46.7 percent. In 1975, there were talks in London to produce a new constitution. Seychelles was to become an autonomous colony, with a coalition government: a year later, a new constitution was finalised.

Independence to the Present

In June 1976, Seychelles became an independent republic in the Commonwealth. The flamboyant Mancham became President, with Rene as Prime Minister. On 5 June 1977, with Mancham in London, the SPUP led an armed coup. A new government was formed, with Rene as President. Seychelles became a one party socialist state and the spup became the sole political party under the title of the Seychelles Peoples Progressive Front (SPPF).

Following the June 1977 coup, Mancham claimed he had no ambitions to return if this meant additional fighting. Other opponents of Rene were not so reticent. In May 1978, 21 Seychellois were arrested for plotting a counter-coup. Among them was Gerard

Hoareau, who was imprisoned for nine months. On release, he left the country and became the chief architect of the *Mouvement Pour La Resistance* which surreptitiously distributed anti-government leaflets and plotted Rene's overthrow.

Rene survived several coup attempts, including a much-publicised one by mercenaries in November 1981. Rumours of an imminent counter-coup persisted. Hoareau remained determined to topple Rene. Three years later, Hoareau was shot dead as he stepped out from his London home. The crime was never solved, but he became a martyr to the cause of the opposition.

In December 1991, Rene announced a return to multi-party politics. Mancham returned to a rousing welcome, but it was Rene who won the majority of the seats at a referendum held in July 1992 to elect a committee to draw up a new constitution. However, the SDP, now known as the dp, walked out of the talks, feeling that the SPPF were forcing the pace. The SPPF presented their draft constitution to the electorate in November 1992 but failed to secure the 60 percent of the votes required for adoption. In an unprecedented display of unity, Mancham and Rene declared that it was in the national interest to forgive and forget the past. They worked closely together, both sides making concessions to produce a second draft constitution. This was adopted by referendum in June 1993.

On 23 July 1993, in Seychelles first multi-party presidential election since independence in 1976, Rene defeated Mancham with 59 percent of the votes cast.

Melting Pot

Most Seychellois are Catholics

The Seychellois, as a people, have a short history. They were brought here from diverse backgrounds. Some came from France in search of their fortunes; others were Creoles, born in the colonies. For years, the majority of the population were voiceless slaves from Africa and Madagascar. By the time they were free, the islands were a British colony. This imposed a foreign veneer on the place, and national and indigeneous characteristics were suppressed.

The Seychellois culture involves a merging of European, African and Malagasy elements. This ongoing process is reflected in the Creole language, which, though based largely on French, has African, Malagasy and Arab words, as well as an increasing number of English ones. It originated as a lingua franca by which slaves from different parts of Africa and Madagascar could communicate with each other and with their French masters.

Most Seychellois are Catholics and think a great deal of their faith. Strangely though, this has not stamped out the tradition of loose family ties, with frequent partner changes or cohabiting couples choosing not to get married until fairly late in life.

Again, despite their strong Catholic traditions, there are still traces of ancient magic left, much of which probably came from African and Madagascan tradition. Known as *grigri*, and practiced by sorcerers called *bonnonm* or *bonnfanm dibwa*, this is still not a subject discussed openly. Ceremonies involve many unusual charms, such as playing cards, old tobacco tins, pebbles, mirrors and old coins, as well as chicken bones, herbal extracts and potions. A good sorcerer can cast a spell on someone to influence his judgment, create a love potion, or deal with a troublesome *dondosya* (zombie) or *nanm* (ghost). Such beliefs flourished when the islands were cut off from the world and people had nothing else to do at night but sit in the candlelight and tell stories in hushed voices. Since the advent of the cinema, radio and TV, their power has waned.

Dance and Music

Old instruments such as the bonm and *zez* are rarely seen, but *moutyas* are occasionally held by the light of bonfires; and no one who has seen the sensual dance can doubt its African origins. At one time, shocked government officials and church leaders tried to stamp out the *moutya*, which is a dance and social event all rolled into one. The dance is slow and sensual, although the dancers barely touch each other. The lively *sega*, now the most popular dance of the islands, is a fairly recent arrival. Its origins are African but the Indian Ocean islands have made it very much part of the Creole culture.

The European element is seen in the *kanmtole*; the robust country dances such as the *vals*, *ecossaise*, polka and *pas de quatre*, which are based on French and English courtly dances.

Moutya drummer

The Seychellois Today

Seychelles was a French colony for 45 years. It was British for over 160 years, yet the British influence seems superficial to the casual observer. The Creole language helps give the place its French feel, but the British elements are strongly reflected in the business end of the islands: the law, the institutions and commerce.

Seychellois are at home in both French and British cultures, but they have also looked beyond them. Creole cuisine is enriched by Indian and Chinese elements, brought in by labourers and traders who came to settle here in the 19th century. The latter communities live somewhat apart from mainstream Creole life, but as shop owners, they are central to the commerce in Seychelles.

Historical Highlights

AD851 Possible first indication of Seychelles on Arab charts.

1501 Jean de Nova discovers and names Farquhar (formerly Jean de Nova).

1502 Vasco da Gama passes through the Amirantes. Seychelles is marked on Portuguese charts.

1609 The *Ascension*, a British ship, arrives at Mahé and finds the islands uninhabited.

1690–1720 Pirates based on Madagascar suspected to have frequented Seychelles.

1742 Lazare Picault sent to report on Seychelles for the French.

1744 Picault sent to collect more details. Mahé is named.

1756 Nicholas Morphey sent to claim the islands for France officially. The islands are named Seychelles, after a French minister.

1770 Brayer du Barré sends the first settlers. Most were later evacuated, nearly starving.

1771 The Royal Spice Garden is established on Mahé.

1778 Lieutenant de Romainville and a 15-man garrison take control of the colony. First buildings erected at *L'Etablissement* (Victoria).

1790 Creation of a Colonial Assembly to discuss local administration and the new ideas of the French Revolution.

1794 First Seychelles Capitulation signed by *Commandant* Quincy.

1801 Arrival of 70 political deportees from France.

1812 Seychelles becomes a British colony.

1835 Abolition of slavery in Seychelles. In an attempt to phase ex-slaves gradually into the community, they were apprenticed to their former owners until emancipation.

1839 Full emancipation of slaves.

1841 *L'Etablissement* is renamed Victoria.

1861 Arrival of the first 'liberated Africans'.

1862 The *Avalanche*, a huge landslide falls on Victoria and claims many victims. Production of coconut oil increases.

1899 Record year for exports of vanilla.

1900 King Prempeh of Ashanti exiled to Seychelles by the British; one of a series of political prisoners sent here.

1903 Seychelles becomes a Crown Colony independent of Mauritius.

1926 Electricity and telephone is introduced.

1939 Creation of Seychelles Taxpayers Association, the first opposition to the colonial administration.

1964 Creation of two political parties, the SPUP and SDP.

1965 Creation of a new colony consisting of the islands of Aldabra, Farquhar and Desroches, called the British Indian Ocean Territory.

1967 Introduction of universal adult suffrage.

1970 The first Constitutional Congress. Creation of a Legislative Assembly. At the first election, SDP wins six seats; SPUP wins five.

1971 Opening of the international airport. Tourism becomes by far the most important source of income for Seychelles.

1976 Seychelles becomes an independent republic in the Commonwealth. Creation of a coalition government; James Mancham (SDP) is President and Albert Rene (SPUP) is Prime Minister.

1977 Coup by the SPUP overthrows Mancham's coalition government.

1978 Seychelles becomes a single party state led by the Seychelles People's Progressive Front (SPPF).

1981 An attempt to overthrow Rene by mercenaries led by 'Mad Mike' Hoare fails.

1982 A mutiny in the army is quelled with the help of Tanzanian troops.

1991 A return to a multi-party system is announced.

1992 First draft constitution fails to secure 60 percent of the votes at the referendum.

1993 Second draft constitution is adopted. Rene wins first multi-party presidential election in a three-cornered fight, with 59 percent of the votes. SPPF wins 27 of 33 seats in Congress, with DP taking five and United Opposition one.

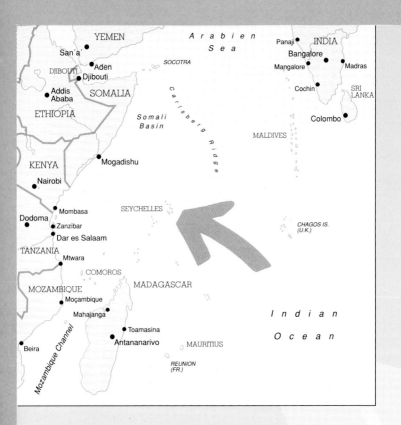

Seychelles and the Indian Ocean

Mahé

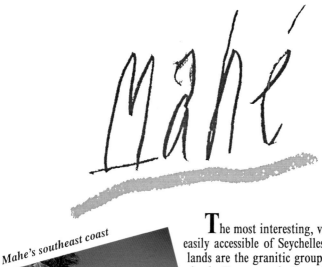

Mahe's southeast coast

The most interesting, varied and easily accessible of Seychelles' 115 islands are the granitic group of 39 islands. Known as the Inner Islands of Seychelles, the main islands in this group are Mahé, Praslin and La Digue. As the Inner Islands lie within a relatively small area, they can be explored using Mahé and Praslin – the two largest islands – as bases.

Wherever you fly from, you will arrive at Mahé, the largest and highest island of Seychelles with an area of 152.6sq km (59sq miles). This is the most developed island, the commercial centre and home to 90 percent of Seychellois. Yet, the mountains are verdant with dense forest, the beaches are superb, and it has the best facilities to enjoy watersports and game fishing.

Many visitors rush away to Praslin, La Digue or even further afield, in the belief they must escape Mahé quickly to discover the real Seychelles. This is a mistake. Mahé is beautiful in its own right and the best base from which to plan excursions to the islands of Frégate and Silhouette, St Anne Marine National Park and other interesting areas.

The stunning Beau Vallon beach is where most tourists stay, yet it is far from crowded. Mass tourism has not arrived in Seychelles. North of Beau Vallon, the coastline is wilder and more rugged. Reclamation along the east coast, between Victoria and the airport, makes this coast less interesting until south of the airport where there are beautiful beaches, most notably Anse Royale.

In the south, Intendance and Takamaka are spectacular beaches, though swimming can be dangerous from May–September. On the west coast, the best swimming is at Anse à la Mouche, sheltered by its wide sweeping corners all year round.

Rainfall in the mountains is double that at the coast, which can make mountain paths slippery, especially during December–Februiary. If you wish to explore the hills, the best time is during the drier, less humid months, from May–September.

The *Day 1 Itinerary* takes you to the best beaches, viewing points, craft centres and the finest of the mountain passes, Sans Souci. This is followed by a selection of *Pick & Mix* options which can be done without checking out of your Mahé hotel. Several of these options can be extended overnight or longer at your leisure.

A car is essential for the full day itinerary on Mahé, and useful for the capital city of Victoria and for the walking tours, though public transport can be used for these trips. Mahé's roads are good, but apart from the new East Coast Highway, are narrow and winding. The Mini Moke is commonly used, although a closed car is more secure if you wish to lock away cameras, watches and other valuables while taking a dip or visiting sites.

DAY ①

From Bel Ombre to Beau Vallon

The plan is for a fairly leisurely full day. You will get to know the island and take in some spectacular scenery. We suggest a quick lunch, making the most of the daylight hours, and taking time over a more lavish dinner. Choose a weekday for your tour as many of the shops in this itinerary which sell crafts close on Sunday. You may wish to return to any of the scenic spots another day.

Ingenious Creole-Chinese cuisine

– This tour sets out from Beau Vallon. If you are staying at the Coral Strand Hotel, or at another hotel north of this hotel, drive towards Victoria as far as Beau Vallon Police Station. Turn right here. If you are staying at Beau Vallon Bay Hotel or Fisherman's Cove, turn right on leaving your hotel and you are on the correct road. From other parts of Mahé, head towards Beau Vallon Police Station and keep on the road towards Bel Ombre. Do not turn down to Beau Vallon Bay itself. If you are staying at any of the west coast hotels, drive north to do the Sans Souci-Beau Vallon section first –

Before setting out, call either **Ty-Foo Restaurant** (Tel: 371485) or **Kaz Kreol Restaurant** (Tel: 371680) to make lunch reservations, and any one of the recommended restaurants in the *Eating Out* sec-

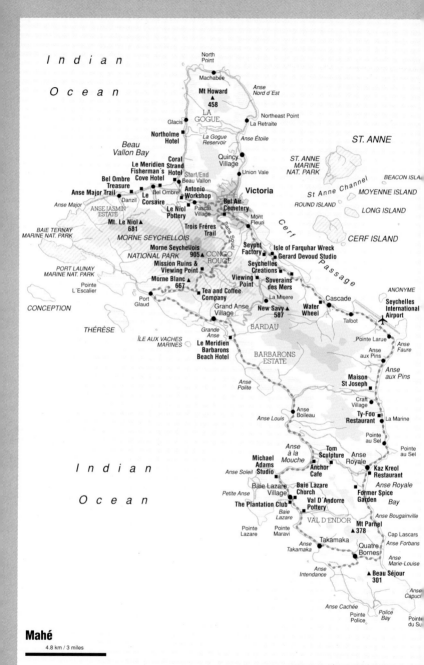

Indian
Ocean

North
Point

Machabée

Anse
Nord d'Est

Mt Howard
458

LA
GOGUE

Glacis

Northeast Point
La Retraite

Anse Étoile

ST. ANNE

Northolme
Hotel

La Gogue
Reservoir

Beau
Vallon Bay

Coral
Strand
Hotel

Quincy
Village

ST. ANNE
MARINE
NAT. PARK

BEACON ISLAND

Le Meridien
Fisherman's Cove Hotel
Start/End
Beau Vallon

Union Vale

Victoria

St Anne Channel

MOYENNE ISLAND

Bel Ombre
Treasure

Anse Major Trail

Danzil

Bel Ombre
Le
Corsaire

Antonio
Workshop

Bel Air
Cemetery

ROUND ISLAND

LONG ISLAND

Anse Major

ANSE JASMIN
ESTATE

Le Niol
Pottery

Pascal
Village

Mont
Fleuri

Cerf

CERF ISLAND

Mt. Le Niol
681

Trois Fréres
Trail

BAIE TERNAY
MARINE NAT. PARK

MORNE SEYCHELLOIS

Passage

Morne Seychellois

Seypot
Factory

Isle of Farquhar Wreck
Gerard Devoud Studio

ANONYME

NATIONAL PARK

905

CONGO
ROUGE

PORT LAUNAY
MARINE NAT. PARK

Mission Ruins &
Viewing Point

Seychelles
Creations

Seychelles
International
Airport

Pointe
L'Escalier

Morne Blanc
667

Viewing
Point

Souverains
des Mers

Cascade

CONCEPTION

Port
Glaud

Tea and Coffee
Company

La Misere

Water
Wheel

THÉRÈSE

Grand Anse
Village

New Savy
587

Talbot

Pointe Larue

Anse
Faure

ÎLE AUX VACHES
MARINES

Grande
Anse

BARDAU

Anse
aux Pins

Le Meridien
Barbarons
Beach Hotel

BARBARONS
ESTATE

Anse Polite

Maison
St Joseph

Anse
aux Pins

Indian

Ocean

Anse
Boileau

Craft
Village

Anse Louis

Ty-Foo
Restaurant

La Marine

Anse
à la
Mouche

Tom
Sculpture

Pointe
au Sel

Pointe
au Sel

Michael
Adams
Studio

Anse Soleil

Anchor
Cafe

Anse
Royale

Kaz Kreol
Restaurant

Petite Anse

Baie Lazare
Village

Baie Lazare
Church

Anse Royale

The Plantation Club

Val D'Andorre
Pottery

Former Spice
Garden

Bay

Baie
Lazare

VAL D'ENDOR

Anse Bougainville

Pointe
Lazare

Pointe
Maravi

Mt Parnel
378

Cap Lascars

Anse Forbans

Takamaka

Quatre
Bornes

Anse
Marie-Louise

Anse
Takamaka

Beau Séjour
301

Anse
Intendance

Anse
Capuci

Anse Cachée

Pointe
Police

Police
Bay

Pointe
du Su

Mahé

4.8 km / 3 miles

tion to reserve a table for dinner. If you have decided on a Chinese lunch at Ty-Foo, try getting there around noon, especially at weekends. Food is always freshly prepared here and you may have a long wait if the restaurant is busy.

Bel Ombre to Bel Air: After 1½km (1 mile) along the Bel Ombre road, you pass **Le Corsaire Restaurant** which offers upmarket dining, (Tuesday–Sunday 7.30– 10pm, closed Monday) on the right.

With small boats anchored inside the breakwater protecting the attractive thatched restaurant building, this is a good place for a photograph.

Bel Ombre pirate treasure dig

After a further 200m (220yds), you reach the fascinating site of Seychelles' most famous **treasure dig** at Bel Ombre. The 18th-century French pirate Olivier Le Vasseur was supposed to have buried his share of the loot – gold and silver bars, strings of pearls, some 5,000 golden guineas, 42 diamonds and the jewel-encrusted regalia of the Archbishop of Goa, which included a large cross studded with rubies – from a Portuguese treasure ship somewhere in this area. Reginald Cruise-Wilkins, a former British big game hunter from Kenya, began the dig at Bel Ombre in the 1960s and his family steadfastly continue the search till today. It is believed that Le Vasseur laid out the site like a vast gaming board based on Greek mythology, and anyone in pursuit of his treasure has to perform the Twelve Labours of Hercules to reach it. The final step, a descent into the underworld, involved excavating an underwater cavern, which explains the sea walls and pumping equipment you can see on the site today.

Carry on to **La Scala Restaurant** (see *Eating Out*) where the road widens and it is easy to turn around and return the way you came. Pass the junction by the Beau Vallon Police Station and continue towards Victoria: there is a petrol station on your right. Chances are your hired car will be delivered to your hotel with an almost empty tank. As this is the last petrol station for a long while on this route, take the opportunity to fill up; 15 litres (3.3 gallons) will be enough.

Antonio the wood sculptor

Just after the first sharp left-hand bend, as you begin to climb the hill towards St Louis, is a sign on the right for the home and workshop of sculptor **Antonio** (open daily 8.30am–5pm). He works in wood and the workshop is well worth a visit if you are interested in sculpture.

After a series of bends, the road

straightens out and there is a sign pointing to a turning to the right for **Le Niol Pottery** (open daily 8.30am–5pm), which is 500m (550yds) along this road. Take the turning and visit the small pottery works of Gordon Robert (Tel: 266107). Robert's best-selling line are his tortoises, but he also has a range of other souvenirs. Return to the main road to Victoria, continuing in the direction of town.

Look out for Hertz Car Hire, followed by a sign for Marlboro cigarettes at the bottom of the hill, and take the next turning to the right, Bel Air Road.

A short distance along Bel Air Road, where it bears to the right, is a bus stop on the left. Immediately after this is a wall with a gateway to the **Bel Air Cemetery**. This is a national monument, though rather overgrown and neglected now. Graves here date from the earliest settlement. Jean-François Hodoul, a corsair based in Seychelles who harried English shipping during the Napoleonic Wars is buried here, as is the so-called Seychelles 'Giant' – his grave marked by an **obelisk** – who according to legend was nearly 3m (9ft) tall. He is supposed to have been murdered by other settlers who were afraid of his great strength. Some graves are made from imported volcanic rocks from Mauritius, others of local beach rock.

Continue uphill, looking out for a sign on the right indicating Pension Bel Air. Shortly after this, there is a phone box on the left; turn here into **Liberation Road**. Soon an excellent view of Victoria, the yacht basin, port and St Anne Marine Park opens up on

View of Victoria from Liberation Road

your left. This is another good photographic stop. This back way around Victoria is worth remembering if you have to pass through town during rush hour, or on Saturday mornings when cars attempt to park where no space exists and a stream of pedestrians who cross the road choke up the one-way system. Continue to the next T-junction and turn right; this direction signposted 'Plaisance 2, Airport 10, South Mahé'.

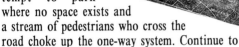

La Misère viewing point

Victoria to Anse Royale: Continue to the next roundabout, known as La Misère Roundabout, and turn right, heading up the hill. After 2km (1¼ miles), look out for a **viewing point** on the left. Turn into this lay-by. A ceramic signboard helps you to pick out the islands in the distance. The view encompasses the islands of St Anne Marine National Park, Praslin (on the horizon) and its satellites, and several other islands. The flat area spread out before you is reclaimed land, as is the airstrip to your right. The dramatic hillside to your right was made famous in a Tarzan film when our hero fell off this hill and discovered a lost world populated by African wild animals. Today, a brewery has been built at the base of this cliff. Return by the same route to the La Misère roundabout and turn right.

After ½km (¼ mile), you reach **Seypot Pottery** (Monday–Friday 8am–4pm, Saturday 8am–noon, closed Sunday) on the right. Immediately on the left is the rotting hulk of the **Isle of Farquhar** inter-island schooner, which now lies land-locked by the reclaimed land of the east coast, followed by the gallery of French painter **Gerard Devoud** (Monday–Friday 8am–4pm, Saturday 8am–noon, closed Sunday).

Continue on past Seychelles Breweries. Just after Chelle Plastics factory is a turning to the right to **Seychelles Creations** (Monday–Friday 8am–noon, 1–4pm, closed Saturday and Sunday) and **Kreol'Or** (Monday–Friday 8am–noon, 1–4pm, closed Saturday and Sunday), two companies which create quality jewellery and souvenirs. Seychelles Creations uses mainly polished coconut wood, shells and other local woods with some tortoiseshell for their work while Kreol'Or uses a lot of tortoiseshell. Do not buy tortoiseshell products. Apart from the moral issue of trading in endangered species like the hawksbill turtle, it is illegal to take tortoiseshell products into over a hundred countries worldwide.

Drive back down to the main road and turn right to continue southwards. Immediately after the British Motors garage on the right is **Souverains des Mers** (Monday–Friday 8am–5pm, closed

Saturday and Sunday), makers of fine quality model boats which range in price from a few hundred rupees to more than the cost of your air ticket to Seychelles.

Continuing southwards, immediately after the Cascade Telephone Exchange on the right, is Seychelles' only **water wheel**. Built in 1910, its original purpose was to power coir and rope making ma-

Maison St Joseph

chinery: today it turns for effect only. The rocks to the left of the water wheel are often draped in washing, the area being a sort of launderette for the locals.

Drive past the airport, past **Katiolo Restaurant and Discotheque** (see *Nightlife*), through Anse aux Pins village and past the Reef Hotel with the golf course just opposite the hotel. About 1km (½mile) past the hotel is the Creole Institute at **Maison St Joseph**. This is a lovely example of an old style Seychellois plantation house.

After a further 500m (550yds) is a sign indicating the **Craft Village** (Monday–Friday 9am–4pm) and **Pomme Cannelle Restaurant** (Tuesday–Sunday, closed Monday, lunch only). There are shops at the Craft Village selling paint-

Craft Village store

ings – including excellent originals of plants and fish by English-born artist Liz Rouillon – T-shirts and beachwear in colourful designs, and other souvenirs, including the inevitable tortoiseshell products. Weekend opening is erratic and the village is usually deserted on Sunday. The restaurant serves ex-

cellent, if somewhat expensive Creole food, and even more expensive meat dishes.

Return to the main road where it is a further 700m (770yds) to the Ty-Foo restaurant (open daily noon–3pm, 6.30–10pm). The service here is a bit slow, but the chef is a genius at whipping up Creole-Chinese cuisine. An alternative choice for lunch is Kaz Kreol (open daily 11am–10pm) at the next village, **Anse Royale**, opposite the petrol station. Kaz Kreol specialises in local cuisine so fish and seafood are therefore heavily featured, but they also

Granite outcrops at Anse Royale beach

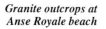

have good meat dishes. The location is beautiful; the restaurant being right on the beach.

Between the two restaurants, but nearer to Ty-Foo, is **La Marine** (Monday–Friday 7.30am–5pm, Saturday 8am–3.30pm, closed Sunday and public holidays), another model boat workshop.

Anse Royale to West Coast: After lunch, continue southwards past Seychelles Polytechnic at Anse Royale. Another 900m (1,000yds) after the polytechnic is a church with the sign '1931. St Joseph. *Patron Des Ouvriers'*. Almost opposite the church is a turning, **Sweet Escott Road**, which leads to the site of the **Royal Spice Garden**. This was the spot where the French tried to grow spices in the early days of settlement, hoping to break the Dutch monopoly of these valuable commodities. Only cinnamon has been at all successful. Today, there is little to see and the garden is overgrown and forgotten, a pity given that Seychelles has so few historic sites.

Do not continue up Sweet Escott Road but continue to Anse Marie-Louise and follow the road inland to **Quatre Bornes**. Here, opposite the police station, is a turning signposted to '**Intendance**'. This is a good and relatively secluded beach to visit but do not try to swim here unless it is calm, especially during the southeast monsoon from April to October. If you have the slightest doubt, give it a miss. Turning left, follow the Intendance road for about 1½km (1 mile) until you meet a turning to the right. Take this turning and follow the track to the beach.

On returning to this junction, it is tempting to follow the road southwards and go in search of even wilder pastures, having experienced the wild beauty of Intendance. Don't bother; there is a prison at the southern extreme of Mahé and a barrier across the road to deter tourists. Return to Quatre Bornes and turn left at the police station, heading downhill to **Takamaka**. Though the beach

itself is picturesque, there are dangerous currents here.

The road now bends northwards, rounding a rocky point (Pointe Maravi) to **Baie Lazare**. Just after the road turns to the left – to pass close by the sandy shore – is a **monument** which commemorates the 250th anniversary of the first official French landing on Mahé by Lazare Picault in 1742.

Baie Lazare church

Continue past Flocy's Store, noting **Baie Lazare Church** on the hill at the northern end of the bay. Descending to **Anse aux Poules Bleues**, the **Michael Adams Studio** is on the left (Monday–Friday 9am–4pm, Saturday 9am–noon, closed Sunday and public holidays) which exhibits paintings by one of Seychelles' most celebrated artists, Michael Adams.

Return to the coast road and continue northwards to the next bay, **Anse à la Mouche**. This is the perfect place for a swim when the tide is in; the bay is calm and sheltered at all times of year and never crowded. The **Anchor Cafe** (open daily 11am–10pm) serves snacks and drinks at good prices.

Take the first turning to the right after Anchor Cafe, **Les Canelles Road**, and drive 800m (½ mile) to visit the studio of sculptor, Tom Bowers. This is on the right, the turning indicated by a signboard: '**Tom Sculpture Studio**'. Return to the coastal road after your visit and turn right. After 7km (4½miles) on a long straight stretch of road is the **Indian Ocean Nurseries** (Monday–Friday 7am–4pm, Saturday 7–11am). Also known as the Orchid Farm, this is the best place to buy orchids should you wish to take some home as souvenirs or gifts. They cost a fraction of the price charged at other locations in Seychelles.

Carry on along the coastal road, past the bbc Indian Ocean Relay Station, ignoring the turning to the right near here. Take the next major right hand turning after a further 4km (2½ miles) in Port Glaud. This is the **Sans Souci Road**, marked by the Port Glaud Police Station on the right and the Ministry of Health clinic on the left.

Sans Souci to Beau Vallon: Sans Souci is the highest and most spectacular mountain pass, with the best views and a lush forest. Most of the road lies in the **Morne Seychellois National Park**. As the road winds upwards, the best spot for a photograph of the west coast is after 1.8km (1 mile).

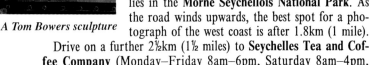

A Tom Bowers sculpture

Drive on a further 2½km (1½ miles) to **Seychelles Tea and Coffee Company** (Monday–Friday 8am–6pm, Saturday 8am–4pm, closed Sunday. This is a good place for a refreshing drink.

A short distance after the tea factory, note the signboard on the left marking the start of the walk to the summit of **Morne Blanc**, (see *Activities*). About 2½km (1½ miles) after the tea factory is another signboard for **Mission Historical Ruins and Viewing Point**.

Turn left here and park at the top. It is well worth the visit for the view and the eerie silence beneath a magnificent avenue of trees leading up to the viewing lodge. The atmosphere at the Mission is unique in Seychelles, far removed from the happy-go-lucky, everyday's-a-holiday feel of the coast. The ruins, dating from 1875, are that of a school built by missionaries to educate the children of liberated slaves in the last century.

Return to the Sans Souci road, over the summit. Note the start of another walk, on the right hand side to **Copolia**, followed about 1km (½ mile) later by another footpath signposted to **Trois Frères** to the left. To get a super view of the east coast and about half of the granite islands, take the **Trois Frères Trail** turning, keeping your fingers crossed that no car will come downhill on this steep, narrow track. It is unlikely, unless of course someone just ahead of you is using this book! Park at the top and the view is laid out before you. The walk, if you return to do it, starts from this car park.

Back to the main road, and after 1½km (1 mile) you pass the residence of the American ambassador on the right, the drive flanked by white pillars. The house is now called **1776** but was known as *Sans Souci* before. Archbishop Makarios was an involuntary resident here in the 1950's when the British exiled him from Cyprus.

Nearly 2km (1 mile) after the embassy residence, look out for a turning to the left, signposted for the residence of the British High Commissioner. Take this turning. Brace yourself for a double hairpin bend even tighter than those on the Sans Souci Road. A short distance further on you will pass the Russian Embassy and reach a T-junction. Turn right, then left at the next T-junction soon after, returning to Beau Vallon and Bel Ombre via this route.

If you wish to continue to Victoria, ignore the British High Commission turning, carrying on to the end of the Sans Souci Road. Turn right at the T-junction for the town centre.

Mission Ruins framed by sangdragon trees at Morne Seychellois National Park

PICK & MIX

1. Victoria and Botanical Gardens

Visit Victoria's Botanical Gardens and see the flora of the tropics. The capital city of Victoria is the heart of Seychelles, where past history and present culture can be sampled. Mornings are best; it is cooler for walking, there is more produce in the market and the flora is at its best. Avoid Saturday – too crowded – and Sunday – just the opposite, almost everywhere is closed! A half day will cover this.

Pretty lily

– Drive to the Botanical Gardens (open daily 6am–6pm), or take a bus to Victoria (a signboard on the bus states the itinerary) and walk out of town along Francis Rachel Street. The gardens are situated on the Mont Fleuri Road, about 300m (1,000ft) after Le Chantier Roundabout (with a statue of a sailfish in the centre). The entrance is on the right just before the turning up to the hospital, and the car park is immediately to the right, inside the gate –

There is a kiosk next to the car park where a useful leaflet to the gardens can be picked up. Walk uphill past an avenue of palms. Ignore the next turning on the right. Just after this on the right is the indigenous coco de mer palm laden with its strange nuts. If you are not planning to visit the Vallée de Mai on Praslin where the coco de mer grows wild, step up for a closer look. Just behind is a pen full of giant land tortoises.

About 50m (165ft) further uphill, cut across the grassy area on your right. There is an aviary to the left housing the pretty Seychelles blue pigeons, while on the right are pools with water plants and a pair of flamingoes. Cut between the pools and head for the

Entrance to the Botanical Gardens

Sapin Restaurant (Monday–Saturday 9am–5pm, closed Sunday) for a cool drink. Return via the steps on the far right, behind the restaurant, descending back to the car park (feel free to invent your own route through the trees and across the grounds).

Clock Tower

Exit the gardens, turn left onto the main road and take the first turning off Le Chantier roundabout. This is Francis Rachel Street, which used to be the coastal road before the land to your right was reclaimed. The National Library is the big building to your right. Beyond it you will see the Cable & Wireless Building on the left. Look out just before this for **Kenwyn House**, a traditional style house owned by the company, set back from the road. A little further on the left, set well back, is Victoria's only **mosque**. Turn right just after this and park at the **Stadium Car Park**.

Set off on foot, back on to Francis Rachel Street and turn right. Just after the service station is a bust of Pierre Poivre, who fostered the idea of growing spices in Seychelles. Behind, and just beyond is the **Court House**, an elegant colonial-style building. Ahead is the **Clock Tower**, a replica of the one near Victoria Station in London. It was erected in 1903 to commemorate Seychelles' new status as a Crown

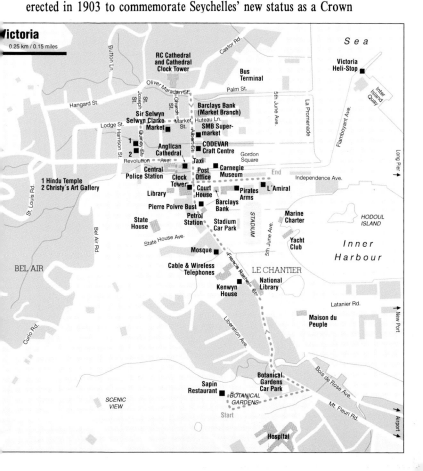

Priests' Residence

Colony independent of Mauritius. Originally black, it has been painted silver.

Cross over the road to the Post Office side and walk straight on to **Albert Street**, past the main taxi stand. Behind the taxi stand is a grassy area called Gordon Square, which was formed from the rubble of a huge landslide in 1862 that claimed many lives. The next building is CODEVAR craft centre (*see Shopping*). Continue to the end of Albert Street, cross over and turn the corner to the left into Oliver Maradan Street. Across this road, steps lead up to the right, into the grounds of the **Roman Catholic Cathedral**.

If you time your visit well and are here on the hour, you will hear the clock that chimes twice, made famous in the title of Alec Waugh's travel book, *Where The Clocks Chime Twice*. It is situated in a clock tower behind the cathedral. It chimes every hour, then again a few minutes later. Beyond the cathedral is the **Priest's Residence**, one of the most elegant buildings in Victoria.

Descend the cathedral steps, cross the road and go down **Church Street**. You cross a small river at this point. It is teeming with tilapia which the Seychellois do not eat, being spoilt for choice by the plethora of marine fish available. Turn right at the next junction into **Market Street**. The **Sir Selwyn Selwyn Clarke Market**, named after a former governor, is ahead to the left. Enter the market and see the fish stalls to the left. Return to Market Street, turn left and walk to the end, about 100m (110yds). There is a small car park on your left, and across the road is Seychelles' only **Hindu Temple**. To the left of the temple is a small supermarket and over the top is **Christy's Art Gallery**, well worth a visit.

From the art gallery, turn right, cross the road and turn left into Revolution Avenue. Cross this road and take the alleyway between Central Police Station and the Anglican Cathedral. Behind these is another stream full of tilapia. Across the car park is a small **Library** (Monday–Friday 9am–5pm, Saturday 9am–noon, closed Sunday), housed in a very attractive balconied building in the colonial style.

From here, go down State House Avenue to the Clock Tower and cross over onto the right-hand side of **Independence Avenue**. Here are stalls selling various souvenirs. Tourists have taught these stallholders how to bargain, a concept that used to be alien to Seychellois, who prefer to offer fixed prices.

Beyond the stalls is Lakaz Boutique des Ar-

Stalls by the Clock Tower

tisans. Across the road is the **Carnegie Museum** (Monday–Friday 8.30am–4.30pm, Saturday 9am–noon, closed Sunday) which houses a collection of cultural and historical items.

Back on the right side, you wil now approach Victoria's two main watering holes; first the **Pirates Arms**, just after Barclays Bank. If you can hold out another 100m (110yds), the second is **L'Amiral** on the corner of **Independence House**, next to the **Tourism Division Shop** where you can collect some reading material whilst you enjoy a snack and a cold drink. Return to the car park via the little road between Barclays and Pirates Arms and walk across the Pirates Arms car park to the Stadium car park.

2. St Anne Marine National Park

See marine life on the coral reef through a subsea viewer without getting wet. You have a choice of making this a full-day trip with swimming, snorkelling and lunch on one of the islands of the St Anne Marine National Park (Moyenne, Round or Cerf). Be forewarned that some tourists have found the enclosed nature of the subsea viewer claustrophobic.

Glass bottom boat

– Trips run daily: Mason's Travel (Tel: 322612) run trips exclusively to Moyenne; and Travel Services Seychelles (Tel: 322414) to Cerf and Round. There is snorkelling gear available on the boats. The cost of the trip to St Anne Marine Park also includes a transfer from your hotel to Marine Charter in Victoria. Pick-up time from west Mahé hotels and Glacis is at 8.15am, Coral Strand 8.30am, and other Beau Vallon hotels 8.40am. Arrive at Marine Charter in Victoria at 9am, and after check in, the glass bottom boat departs at 9.30am. Return to Mahé at around 4pm for the transfer back to your hotel –

The glass bottom boat affords a vertical view of the reef, but it also makes most fish scatter. The guide may amuse you by feeding sergeant major fish by hand, but you really get to see the reef when you transfer to a subsea viewer once within the Marine Park's waters. This is a semi-submersible vessel which allows a horizontal view of the marine life, thereby scaring fewer fish.

Round Island is tiny, and you can walk around it at a leisurely pace in 10 minutes. The beach is excellent for swimming. For snorkelling, there are some good coral heads near the jetty. For a superb lunch, try **Chez Gabby**, the island's only restaurant. On **Moyenne** the snorkelling is better, especially off the edge of the island facing the open ocean, but this is not possible at all times of the year. Occasionally, snorkelling is done off St Anne. Strong

33

An underwater symphony

swimmers can swim from Round to Moyenne. Moyenne also provides a first class lunch. **Cerf** is a much larger island, also with good swimming and more to explore. There are two good restaurants, the **Beach Shed**, where there are giant land tortoises, and the **Kapok Tree**.

The St Anne Marine National Park is showing signs of wear and tear from the increasing numbers of visitors it is receiving. It has also suffered some siltation resulting from reclamation work carried out on the east coast of Mahé. On the other hand, **Baie Ternay Marine National Park** on the west coast is still in very good condition. It is smaller than St Anne, but the number of visitors is correspondingly small too. The best way to visit is by **Teddy's Glass Bottom Boat** (Tel: 261125, or visit his stall opposite the pool bar, Coral Strand Hotel). Trips depart at 10am Saturday (full day) and 2am Monday, Wednesday, Thursday, Friday (half day) and return at 5pm (all days). Full-day trips include a barbecue lunch at **Anse du Riz**.

The trip to Baie Ternay is along a rocky coast looking up at the dramatic peak of Morne Seychellois. Apart from the extreme southeastern corner, this is the only stretch of Mahé with no coastal road. Long may it remain so!

3. Scenic Flight

See Mahé and its satellite islands from the air. If you have never been up in a helicopter before, don't miss this exhilarating experience. Even if you have, you will find Seychelles from the air spectacular. Only from this vantage point can you really take in the varied shades of the blue sea, the majestic green mountains and the beautiful beaches all at once. If you have an autofocus camera, you may find that the wind rushing past will play havoc with your controls if you poke the lens too far out. Take care

that your spectacles or sunglasses don't get blown away. The flight lasts 30 minutes.

– Scenic flights depart from Victoria Helistop.
The flights also depart from other points around the island, so it is best to enquire with a travel agent or call Helicopter Seychelles (Tel: 275400) –

There are four seats, one next to the pilot and three just behind. The best seats for photography are by either window at the back. These windows have a slot which slides open to enable you to take photographs unimpeded. The co-pilot's seat has a smaller sliding window that photographers may find difficult to crouch down to, but the all-round view is superb for non-photographers.

From the Victoria Helistop, you take off and head out towards the St Anne Marine National Park. The Tuna Quay, yacht basin and commercial port are on your right, and the islands of St Anne – Cerf, Long, Round, Moyenne and Ile Cahée on the left.

Heading southwards, all the flat land you see to the right – traversed by the east coast road – is reclaimed from

Up, up and away!

the sea. The most prominent building is the Unity Stadium, built to host the 1993 Indian Ocean Games.

Next, comes Seychelles International Airport, followed by Anse aux Pins and the beautiful bay of Anse Royale with its picturesque church and modern polytechnic. The helicopter then crosses over to the west coast before reaching the southern tip of Mahé, affording glorious views of the wild bays of Intendance and Takamaka, and the calm sheltered waters of Anse à la Mouche and Anse Boileau.

Heading north, towards the Morne Seychellois National Park, you look down upon solid greenery, broken only by the granite slopes of Morne Blanc, Morne Seychellois and other peaks. Ahead lies Beau Vallon, the main tourist beach. Your pilot then traverses up the northern tip of Mahé and heads back to base. Your whistle-stop tour is over in a flash, but you won't forget it for a long time.

West coast of Mahé from the air

4. Silhouette and North Islands

Spend a day visiting two beautiful islands with no roads. Different from the granite islands, these are volcanic in origin. The old way of plantation life still continues on Silhouette – the third largest island after Mahé and Praslin – while North has all the fascination of an island now abandoned.

La Passe jetty at Silhouette

– There is a small, expensive hotel on Silhouette, 19km (12 miles) northwest of Mahé, but day trips by boat are possible. These can be arranged through Travel Services Seychelles Ltd (Tel: 322414). The Mancienne brothers (Tel: 247382 or 247898), whose premises, The Boat House, is on Beau Vallon beach, offer more flexibility and cater for smaller parties. Trips depart at 9am and return at 6pm. The boats leave from opposite The Boat House –

Wear your swimsuit or shorts and shoes you can slip off easily. Flip flops are easy to slip on and off and are adequate for walking ashore, unless you plan any major ascents of Silhouette's steep mountains. There is some shade on the boat but take along sun screen and a hat (one which will not blow off easily), and use both. Plenty of soft drinks are available on the boat – included in the cost of the trip – as is the use of fishing gear, the landing fee for Silhouette and a barbecue lunch.

The format of the Manciennes' day trip is flexible and usually includes trawl fishing in each direction if customers are interested. This is also a good way of making sure that the fish for the barbecue is fresh! If you prefer to simply get to the islands and spend as much time ashore as possible, discuss this first with the Manciennes and they will try to team you up with others of like mind, rather than a group of ardent fishermen. Landings are usually made only on **Silhouette**, the boat doing a very interesting circuit around the coast of North, or anchoring off North for a spot of snorkelling. If you wish to land on both islands, you should also discuss this in advance.

You first board a small inflatable boat for the transfer to the larger boat which will take you across to the island. Assuming you do not spend too much time fish-

Beachside house, Silhouette

Swaying palms and limpid waters – North Island view from Silhouette

ing, you will arrive at Silhouette by about 11am. A small boat from the island will come out to the anchorage and ferry you ashore to a stone jetty at **La Passe**. There should be time to explore a little before lunch. It is a good idea to have a drink before setting off.

Set back from the beach is a lovely **plantation house**, now empty though well maintained. This is the house of the wealthy Dauban family who used to own Silhouette till about 1983.

Follow the track to the left into the small group of wooden houses. On the right is an old *kalorifer*, where coconuts were dried to make copra. The track climbs upwards through a gate and around a marsh to the right, which is now planted as

The Dauban Mausoleum

a garden area. Beyond, framed by tall coconut palms, is Seychelles' strangest monument, the **Dauban Mausoleum** – built to resemble a small Greek temple.

Continue over the hill and descend to the shore to Anse Cimitière and immediately beyond that to **Anse Lascars**. As you descend, there is a spectacular slope of volcanic syenite to your right. At the far side of Anse Lascars, at the top of the beach, are graves which are said to be Arabic in origin. Just beyond this beach is **Pointe Zeng Zeng**, the only place in Seychelles where black volcanic cinders can clearly be seen. Return to La Passe for your simple barbecue lunch by the beach.

Silhouette rises to 740m (2,400ft), though 65 million years ago it was an enormous volcano rising to about 3,000m (10,000ft). The high forest contains many of Seychelles' unique plants, but to reach the best areas requires a long and sometimes difficult walk. There is an easier track which goes over a low pass in the hills. The starting point of this track is behind the houses to the right as you walk off the jetty. If you are still feeling energetic after lunch, this will give you some idea of Silhouette's interior, but don't expect to conquer the summit in an afternoon. Take it easy, and allow yourself plenty of time to get back for the time arranged with the boatman. There is a picturesque church en route to the path.

Alternatively, you could take a stroll along the beach to **Anse la Passe**, but keep clear of the hotel compound about 500m (550yds) north of the jetty as this is for hotel guests only.

Time permitting, and if you have arranged it in advance, you will leave for **North Island** by about 3pm. About 201ha (497 acres) in size, the sail around North is fascinating. The colours of the rocks (North is composed of syenite like Silhouette), the high ledges where endemic screwpines grow, the spectacular *glacis* (granitic rock slopes) falling away into the sea and the caves eked out over centuries by the licking of the waves are breathtaking and photogenic. There is a lovely beach in the centre of each side of the island, once a thriving plantation. This is now deserted; the fruit trees laden with fruit which is never harvested.

The time to return depends on whether you want to fish on the way back or not. You will probably linger ashore as long as possible, unless the main object of your trip was the fishing, so the best plan is to leave North or Silhouette – if you have remained here – at around 4.30pm to arrive back at Beau Vallon about 6pm.

5. Starlight Cruise

Cruise around Mahé's rocky northern coast as the sun sets; enjoy local music and dancing with dinner on tiny Round Island. The trip takes a full evening, returning to Victoria after 10pm.

– Trips run on Wednesdays, weather permitting, by Travel Services Seychelles (Tel: 322414). Cost includes a pick up from hotels at around 4pm for departure at 5pm –

Starlight cruise entertainment

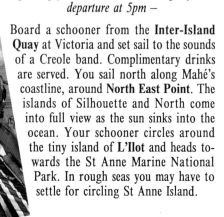

Board a schooner from the **Inter-Island Quay** at Victoria and set sail to the sounds of a Creole band. Complimentary drinks are served. You sail north along Mahé's coastline, around **North East Point**. The islands of Silhouette and North come into full view as the sun sinks into the ocean. Your schooner circles around the tiny island of **L'Ilot** and heads towards the St Anne Marine National Park. In rough seas you may have to settle for circling St Anne Island.

Beach barbecue

By the time you reach Round Island, it will be dark. Disembark via a shallow draft glass bottom boat. The tempo moves up a beat with the strong drumbeats of a *moutya* band.

Dinner is a barbecue with fish steaks, chicken and other dishes served within a stone's throw of the beach, under an open-sided shelter with tables and chairs. Afterwards, there is more music and dancing, and you are invited to join in. The idea is to dance the *sega*, but most just wiggle their bottoms and shuffle their legs in a vague approximation. It doesn't much matter what you do, but prizes are awarded to those who come closest.

6. Frégate

The most easterly island of Seychelles is a verdant plantation island with beautiful beaches, clear blue waters, one of the rarest birds on earth and some intriguing legends about its first settlers, the pirates. This is a full-day trip.

— Frégate is reached by a 15-minute flight from the Inter-Island Terminal at the International Airport, Mahé. Flights depart daily (except Monday) at 10am and return at 4pm. There is one guest house: Frégate Island Plantation House. Enquire at your hotel desk or travel agent for details. The island is usually closed to visitors for about three weeks around Christmas and New Year. Bookings can be made through a travel agent or at the Frégate office in Shipping House, Revolution Avenue, Victoria (Tel: 224789). The cost of the day trip includes lunch —

A Seychelles magpie robin

You will be met by the **Plantation House** manager on arrival and escorted to the hotel's entrance (through the roots of a giant banyan tree) to assemble for a guided tour which is worth doing to get your bearings. The tour takes less than an hour, following the pathway around the Plantation House. You are familiarised with the various crops growing in the plantation, the birds and the giant land tortoises, but the tour doesn't take you to any of the sites really, since these are much further afield.

While on the tour you will come across the Seychelles magpie robin. Extinct on the other granite islands where it was once common, this bird is the symbol of Frégate, where 24 or so magpie robins survive. A reintroduction programme to start a second population on the island of Aride is now under way.

If you decide to continue exploring after the tour, the best place to find magpie robins is on the pathway behind the Plantation House and around the plantation. Sometimes, they put in a guest appearance on the lawn in front of the hotel.

Shell collage in church, Frégate

There are three other paths radiating from the Plantation House that are worth exploring. For the best snorkelling, take the path to the southeast of the island (away from the airstrip) to **Anse Parc**. The walk takes only about 10 minutes. Close to the beach a sign points to the right, to the **Pirate's Wall**. To us it looks more like a stockade than any sort of housing foundation, and no one seems to have ruled out a possible Arab origin, but early stories of pirates abound on Frégate. It is said that in 1812, a gold shoulder strap and cross belt was found here. Other reported finds were a lead-lined well, three coral tombs on which sword hilts were laid, scattered bones and other old walls. These include some little-visited walls on **Signal Hill**, the highest point on Frégate at 125m (410ft) in the northwest of the island.

To reach **Anse Victorin**, the most beautiful beach and the best one for swimming, start from the Plantation House and take the path that runs inland at an angle from the airstrip. Cross the Bamboo River and continue to the coast. At a leisurely pace, the walk takes about 30 minutes.

A third walk along a well-marked track heading inland from the plantation heads due west to Grand Anse, another beautiful beach. As you approach **Grand Anse**, the hill to the left is called **Au Salon**. Here, sangdragon trees grow, and if you look closely, you may see giant tenebrionid beetles clinging to the bark, a species unique to Frégate. It is said that when the first specimens were sent back to Europe, scientists refused to believe these bizarre creatures were genuine as they appeared to be made up from parts of a number of different insects. The walk to Grand Anse takes about 20 minutes.

Keep your eye on your watch and remember to return to the Plantation House by 3.30pm. While waiting for your plane, the small **church** next to the Plantation House is worth a look to see the collages made from seashells.

40

PRASLIN

Praslin, though the second largest island of Seychelles with an area of 27 1/2 sq km (10½ sq miles), is a big step back in time from Mahé. The roads are in poorer condition than Mahé's, but the hotels are as good. There are two main centres for tourists: one on the west coast at Grand Anse (just south of the airport which links the island to Mahé), and the other at Anse Volbert, on the opposite side.

Praslin's beaches are even better than Mahé's, with the southern section from Grand Anse to Baie Ste Anne by far the best. This section also has some accommodation, but is largely undeveloped, unspoilt and picturesque.

Baie St Anne, in the southeast corner, is a natural sheltered harbour. Here, the ferries depart and arrive on weekdays, linking Praslin with the islands of Mahé and La Digue.

The jewel of Praslin is the World Heritage Site of the Vallée de Mai, which lies within the Praslin National Park. A pilgrimage to this unique palm forest, where the strange coco de mer grows, is included in the *Day 1 Itinerary*. The island tour is best done by car — or better yet, by jeep — if it is to be completed in a day. Be forewarned that some of the roads are very rough (especially after rain). Check the brakes before you set off, as rental cars are not always in the best of condition.

Boat trips from Praslin are the best way to see the smaller satellite islands of Praslin, including Cousin and Curieuse, and a little further afield, the best preserved island and finest nature reserve of the granitic islands, Aride. All these are covered as day trips in the *Pick & Mix* section, several of which can be extended overnight.

Praslin's shores are blessed with beautiful beaches

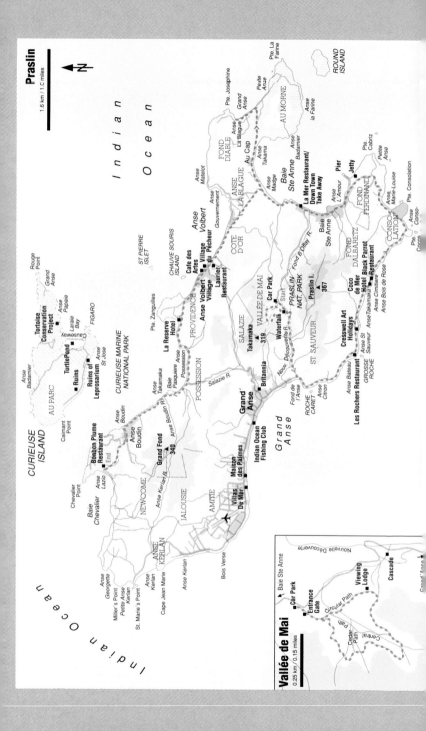

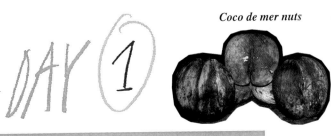

Coco de mer nuts

DAY 1

Vallée de Mai to Anse Lazio

Visit the Vallée de Mai National Park to see the unique palm forest and the black parrot, Seychelles' national bird; then take the most beautiful coastal drive in Seychelles. A fairly busy morning and relatively lazy afternoon. You may wish to re-visit some of the beaches on another day.

— To reach the starting point from Grand Anse or Praslin Airport, drive south (turn left at the junction of the airport road). Beyond the village, the main road turns left, uphill and inland. The Vallée de Mai is 2km (1¼ miles) up the hill. From Anse Volbert, drive south to Baie Ste Anne and turn right at the only junction with a major road, just after Barclays Bank. From Anse St Sauveur, drive north towards Grand Anse and take the first turning on the right. Fill up at Grand Anse or Baie Ste Anne Service Station (10 litres will be sufficient) —

Park at the **Vallée de Mai** car park and purchase your entry ticket to the park (daily 7.30am–5.30pm) from the kiosk. It is also well worth buying the booklet *Vallée de Mai* by Katy Beaver and Lindsay Chong Seng. The wealth of information will add to your appreciation of this magnificent forest. Arrive early if you can. It is cool in the forest for most of the day, but the atmosphere is better enjoyed before the larger tourist groups arrive at mid-morning.

There is an **Information Centre** with souvenirs, snacks and drinks on sale. It is worth taking at least something to drink with you. Fruit juices in cartons are lightest, but don't forget to dispose of the containers properly.

Young coco de mer plants

The paths in the park are well-marked but are unpaved, uneven and have some steep steps. Climb the steps to the right of the car park entrance. From the entrance, follow the numbered trail. It is worth doing the whole **Circular Path** at a leisurely pace, allowing two or three hours for the walk.

There are numerous young coco de mer trees at the start of the trail. There are separate male and female trees but at this age it is impossible to tell them apart. The leaf petiole is the largest of any plant in the world but it is the double coconut from the female tree, the world's largest seed, that has made the tree famous. It is the shape – suggestive of the female pelvis – together with the equally suggestive shape of the male catkin that fascinates many non-botanists.

You will see mature male and female trees further into the valley, especially between **posts 6** and **7**. It takes about 15 years before a trunk develops and another 20–40 years before the tree reaches maturity while the nuts take seven years to develop. Trees may live for over 200 years, reaching some 32m (104ft) in height; males being much taller than females. Nuts may weigh 20kg (44lbs) and a tree can bear up to 35 nuts at a time, weighing up to an an incredible 700kg (1540lbs) in total. There are some particularly old trees around trail **posts 11** and **12**.

The British general, Charles Gordon, who is famous for his dramatic death during the defence of Khartoum, visited Seychelles in 1881 and was deeply impressed by the Vallée de Mai. He was a religious man and a serious thinker, and concluded that Seychelles was the actual site of the legendary Garden of Eden. He went on to write a lengthy treatise on the subject, in which he proposed that the coco de mer was the Tree of Knowledge, and the breadfruit the Tree of Life.

The Vallée de Mai has examples of all six palms unique to Seychelles scattered throughout the area, but trail **post 5** is a good place for an overall appraisal of the river valley.

Apart from palms, the Vallée de Mai is also famous as the home of the Seychelles black parrot. You may hear their whistles almost anywhere but not see the birds because of the dense vegetation. The best places to look are near the entrance, along the roadside and from the northern viewpoint, close to **post 10**, where there is a shelter and benches. This is a good place to take a break and keep your eyes peeled. Return to the car park via the Circular Path.

Another postcard pretty beach, this one at Anse Takamaka

Vallée de Mai to **Anse Lazio**: From the car park, turn right and head towards **Grand Anse**. In just under 1km (½ mile), there is a lovely **waterfall** framed by endemic palms on the right. At the bottom of the hill, turn left (signposted 'Anse Consolation'). From this point to Baie Ste Anne, we think, is the most beautiful coastal car drive in Seychelles. There are eight bays, each one extremely photogenic.

First is **Anse Citron**, then **Anse Bateau**, at the far end of which is **Les Rochers Restaurant** (see *Eating Out*), considered by some to be the finest restaurant in Seychelles.

Another 750m (825yds) further on the right is **Cresswell Art Holidays**, the lovely new building surrounded by flame trees. Verney Cresswell, a British-born artist, offers not just an art gallery with originals and prints of typical Seychelles scenes and some abstracts, but also lessons in art at very reasonable prices. This is a good way to spend a rainy day on Praslin, or to get a new perspective on the sights once you have covered them by car.

Beyond this point is **Anse Takamaka**, then **Anse Cimitiére** on the point of which is the **Black Parrot Restaurant** (see *Eating Out*).

All these bays are good for a swim, though you may have to wade quite far out at low tide. Rounding **Pointe Cocos**, Anse Consolation is less ideal for swimming, due to the beach rock barrier here. The rock, which looks like fossilised coral, is formed where fresh river water mixes with sea water, causing calcareous materials to solidify.

Around **Pointe Consolation** is **Anse Marie Louise**, the best beach on this stretch of coast for a swim and a particularly quiet and picturesque spot. From the beach, the road winds steeply upwards to round **Point Cabriz** before descending equally steeply to Baie Ste Anne. The area to the left is **Fond Ferdinand**, a mainly coco de mer forest, slowly recovering from a major bush fire in 1990.

Building a boat

Turn left at the T-junction, pass the **boat yard** to your right and service station on the left; continue past the post office, market, community centre and ignore the major left turning (back to the Vallée de Mai). Just beyond this junction on the right is the cheap but clean and pleasant **La Mer Restaurant** (Monday–Friday 11am–3pm, 6.30–10pm) which adjoins the **Down Town Take Away** – perfect for a takeaway picnic lunch. You waste as little time as possible if you lunch this way, and the food is good and very cheap. If you do decide to do this, drive on out of the village,

about 1km (½ mile), to **Anse Madge**. There is a gap between the trees where you can pull right off the road and park. You can either enjoy your picnic lunch here, or on the very peaceful beach which overlooks Baie Ste Anne to the right. There are no bins provided, so make sure that you take your litter home with you.

Continue on the coastal road. Where this road turns left inland is a track going straight on to **Anse La Blague**. This is an interesting diversion, but the road is steep and deeply potholed. If you take this there-and-back trip, take the hills in first gear. Notice how pink the granite is here. Praslin is famous for this and some Mahé buildings, such as the Maison du Peuple (the parliament of Seychelles), are constructed from this pink granite; its colour caused by the presence of alkaline felspars. Where the road forks, keep right. The bay at the end of the road is little visited, but it can be quite rough during strong north-westerly winds.

Return to the main road and continue in the same direction (signposted 'Anse Boudin 6km'). The road passes through pleasant takamaka and casuarina woodland. Ignore a fork to the left and drive to Anse Volbert. Here on the right is **Village du Pecheur** (open daily, lunch and dinner). If the idea of a takeaway does not appeal, we recommend you try this restaurant; it has an excellent choice of fish and meat dishes at sensible prices.

Alternatively, for good Creole food, try **Laurier Restaurant** (see *Eating Out*), on the opposite side of the road. A little further on is **Cafe des Arts** (Tuesday–Sunday 9am–1pm, 4–8pm, closed Monday), on the right – worth a visit to see the work of local artists. You might wish to have lunch here. Nice surroundings but expensive prices.

Continue northwards on the Anse Boudin road, round Pointe Zanguilles and past the turning to the La Reserve Hotel, emerging back on the coast at **Anse Possession**, where the French staked their claim to the island in 1768. The lead plaque they had laid disappeared within a few years and it was suspected the English had taken it. There was a rumour that it had been tampered with by an officer of an English ship who replaced the name of the French ship with that of his own.

The coast north of here, facing Curieuse Island, is very pretty, quiet, and good for swimming. At Anse Boudin, the road turns inland over the hill to **Anse Lazio**. This used to be a quiet corner of Praslin but has become very popular since **Bonbon Plume Restaurant** (lunch and dinner, closed Monday) opened its doors. The restaurant sells mainly seafood and is fairly expensive. It is still a very pretty bay, with good swimming, but it can be very rough when the wind is north-westerly. Backtrack from here to your hotel.

PICK & MIX

7. La Digue

Possibly the most beautiful granite island of Seychelles, the spectacular La Digue Coast — with its huge boulders towering over perfect beaches — is backdrop to many a glossy magazine advertisement. A small, friendly local population live on the land, thriving on fishing or by boat-building. Old planters' houses and a sleepy pace of life add to the charm. You will need a whole day on La Digue.

— Take a 30-minute ride on the ferry to La Digue from Baie Ste Anne jetty on Praslin, as there is no airstrip. It is usually not a problem getting a seat but to be certain, call the ferry owner,

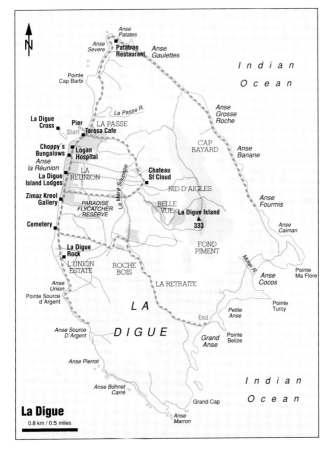

La Digue
0.8 km / 0.5 miles

William Rose (Tel: 233229 or 233874) beforehand, and book yourself on the 9.30am ferry. There are also departures at 7am and 10.30am. Note that the 9.30am ferry does not operate on Sundays. If you do not have a car, ask your hotel to arrange a taxi to the Baie Ste Anne jetty – allow 30 minutes from Grand Anse and 15 minutes from Anse Volbert. Ask the taxi driver to pick you up on your return on the 5.30pm ferry – arriving on Baie Ste Anne at 6pm – since taxis do not always meet the ferries. There is only one taxi on La Digue which usually meets the ferry, if not already on hire –

As there are few vehicles on La Digue, the third largest island at 10 sq km (10½ sq miles), the best way to see it is by bicycle. If you are not a good rider, take care. Some of the tracks are uneven, especially on downhill slopes where rain has made gullies which run off the edge of the road. Make sure you feel comfortable with the bike you hire and that the brakes work. It is possible to do the tour on foot if you are a brisk walker, or you can hire the one and only taxi on the island. Ox cart rides are a novelty but can be tediously slow and a bit uncomfortable as the roads are bumpy and potholed.

Arrival at La Passe

There are restaurants and a cafe on La Digue, as well as shops where you can buy snacks: so unless you prefer to take a packed lunch from your hotel, you need not worry about food until you get there. You arrive at La Passe jetty, near the same point where **La Digue**'s first settlers arrived.

These people were exiled from the Indian Ocean island of Bourbon – now Reunion – after leading a rebellion because they thought the French governors were going to hand Bourbon over to the British. The French plan was to exile the rebels on the Indian coast, but instead, the rebels hijacked the ship and forced the captain to bring them to La Digue. Up to that point, the island had not been successfully settled, perhaps because of the difficult landing. These exiles stuck it out however, and La Digue became one of the most prosperous islands of all, studded with rich plantations.

Note the **Tarosa Cafe** on the right-hand side at the end of the jetty. You may return here for an inexpensive lunch. There is a small **fish market** on the right. There will probably be ox carts waiting to meet tourists booked on a package trip. Ox carts were once the main form of public transport on La Digue, but today

La Digue's eco-friendly transport

Lunch under swaying palms at the Tarosa Café

there are a couple of buses and an increasing number of pick-up trucks. Ox carts are retained just for the tourists.

You will also see plenty of bicycles for hire in this vicinity. On foot, or by bike, set off heading south (turn right on leaving the jetty). Looking out to sea, there is a view of the **La Digue Cross**. This monument was erected on top of granite rocks in the bay in 1931 by Swiss priest Georges Fuffeieux, in memory of people who drowned while attempting to land on La Digue in the past.

A short distance further on the right is the **Logan Hospital**, named after a former British governor of Seychelles. There are a number of traditional houses in this vicinity; two are situated on the right just after **Choppy's Bungalows** (Tel: 234224).

After passing the chalets of **La Digue Island Lodge and Restaurant** (Tel: 234232), take the turning to the left. This road is called **Pont Bill**, or Bill's Bridge. About 200m (220yds) along this road you will reach the **Flycatcher Reserve** on the right. The reserve was initially established by Christopher Cadbury, the chocolate industrialist and nature conservationist, who rented this area of forest from the land owner to preserve one of the best habitats for the Seychelles black paradise flycatcher. Later, the area was acquired by the Seychelles government and given legal protection.

Flycatcher Reserve

The best way to see the flycatcher is to walk along the trails beneath the trees to the far side of the reserve – a point soon reached as the reserve is long but narrow. The male flycatcher is probably the most beautiful of Seychelles' unique birds. Its long black tail gives the bird its local name, vev, meaning widow, because of its 'widow's weeds'.

The flycatchers are almost entirely confined to La Digue – there are just a few birds on Cote d'Or, Praslin – with a population here

49

of about 100. There is tremendous pressure on their habitat from the growing human population and the boat-building industry, but at least local boys have dropped the habit of killing them for sport — thanks to the interest tourists take in La Digue's special bird.

Return to Pont Bill road and continue down this track to the T-junction and turn left. About 200m (220yds) further on you pass **Chateau St Cloud** to your right. This chateau offers by far the cheapest accommodation in Seychelles, although it is not found in the usual tourist literature.

Continue to follow the same road which arches back to rejoin the coastal road near the jetty. Buy a refreshing drink from one of the local shops (most have fridges) or the Tarosa Cafe which sells fresh fruit juices.

Head north along the coastal road. It turns inland to round Cap Barbi and then descends to Anse Sévère. Around the next point is **Anse Patates**, the location of **Patatran Restaurant**. You might like to return here for a Creole lunch at a moderate price. The location is superb, sheltered from prevailing winds which may blow from the northwest or the southeast. It is also an excellent spot for swimming and snorkelling.

Continue around the point of land jutting out into the sea and you reach a wild stretch of coast. In places, wind-blown sand may make cycling difficult. If you see a patch of sand ahead, it is better to disembark; you could be sent flying over the handlebars (we speak from personal experience)! The first bay is **Anse Gaulettes**, a long bay of almost 1km (½ mile), followed by smaller bays, half this size, of **Anse Grosse Roche**, **Anse Banane**, and **Anse Fourmis**, where the track finally peters out. There is a footpath that continues around the next corner, but it is not suitable for bicycles. Turn around and return to Patatran or Tarosa for lunch.

Once refreshed, continue along the coast on the road towards Pont Bill, but this time carry on southwards, following the coast to **L'Union Estate**. Visit **Zimaz Kreol Art Gallery** (Monday–Friday

9am–5pm, Saturday 9am–noon, closed Sunday). Just before L'Union Estate is a small cemetery to the right, by the sea, which is worth a look. Here, some of the earliest settlers on La Digue are buried.

There is a small charge for entering L'Union Estate which produces high grade copra (dried coconut). There is a *kalorifer* for drying the coconut flesh and an oil press — a kind of giant mortar and pestle. The oil is used for various purposes, including cooking and the manufacture of soap, hair oil and sun lotion.

An artistic diversion

Vanilla is also grown here. It was a lucrative crop on La Digue following its introduction around 1866 but the industry crashed about half a century later, mainly due to the development of synthetic vanillin.

Other attractions of the estate include the huge **La Digue Rock** and a few tame giant land tortoises. There is also a **plantation house** which has earned its place in history because one of the infamous *Emmanuelle* films was made in its premises. Follow the road past these various sites until it curls back towards the beach at **Anse Union and Pointe Source d'Argent**. With the sun high in the sky, this could be a good time to simply relax and enjoy a siesta.

harvest of coconuts

Thus revitalised, exit from the estate and take the sharp turning to the right, signposted for **Grand Anse**. The land on either side of the road soon becomes quite marshy. The area is known as **La Mare Soupape**. *Soupap* is the local word for terrapin, and many of these unique Seychelles creatures can be found here.

a Digue's plantation house

Just beyond the marsh, the road bends sharply to the left. The granite rocks immediately on the right at this point are worth a second glance. At a height of nearly 3m (10ft) above the ground, there is a wedge of fossilised beach rock, indicating that the sea level was once higher than it is today.

Just before the road turns uphill, there is a glimpse of the **Grand Anse River**. This is a local launderette of sorts where the women gather to wash their clothes in the river and lay them out on the ground to dry.

Eventually the road heads downhill, with large trees giving some shade. When you reach the beach, however, there is less shade. It can be dangerous to swim here during May–October. Allow about an hour for a leisurely journey back to La Passe for your ferry home – a distance of nearly 5km (3 miles).

8. Aride

Owned and managed by the Royal Society for Nature Conservation (RSNC), the 68-ha (168-acre) Aride is the finest nature reserve of the granitic Seychelles and a conservationist's paradise. It has more breeding species of seabirds than the other 38 granite islands combined, plants found nowhere else on earth and rare endemic land birds. A full-day trip from Praslin.

Landing on Aride

Aride has no jetty. Visiting boats moor offshore and transfer passengers to the island's small boats. Getting ashore calls for visitors to be nimble in disembarking. The island paths are steep, uneven and exposed to the sun in parts.

Weather conditions sometimes make landing difficult. It is best to plan a visit to Aride as early as possible during your stay; if weather conditions are unfavourable, you can reschedule your trip. The island is open to visitors only four days a week: Wednesday, Thursday, Friday and Sunday. If you wish to check in advance on landing conditions, call the Warden at 321600. You should wear shorts or a bathing costume and carry your shoes, as it will be a wet landing on the beach. Cameras, towels and valuables should be carried in a plastic bag as they may be splashed, especially when leaving and heading into the swell.

You should take binoculars if you have one, a sun hat, sun cream and walking shoes (not flip flops as the hill path is rocky and rough). A bottle of water or soft drinks for the hill walk are also useful, but do not weigh yourself down. Soft drinks are provided with lunch by most of the boats which arrange trips to Aride. Bring your own towel, and if you like, snorkelling equipment. Photographers should take plenty of film as both scenery and birds are very photogenic. Lunch is provided on organized trips, otherwise there is no food available on the island.

On arrival, you will transfer to a rigid hull inflatable or a fibreglass boat. Once ashore, a member of staff will point you in the direction of the **Visitors' Shelter** along the beach. When everyone is assembled and has put on their shoes, a guided tour departs from here. Although visitors are allowed to walk alone along the paths of the plateau, they may not climb the hill unescorted. The hillside is riddled with the burrows of wedge-tailed shearwaters, and much damage may be done to both bird and man if visitors wander at will in the forest. At certain times of the year, it is impossible to take tours up the hill because there are so many birds that visitors would cause great disturbance; birds, chicks and eggs could be trodden upon. Tours are done in English, though leaflets are also available in French, German and Italian.

From the Visitors' Shelter, a path cuts through coconut scrub to the coastal forest where you are likely to see one of the island's rarities, the Seychelles warbler. Once almost extinct and confined to Cousin, 29 birds were transferred to Aride in September 1988. Today, there are over 300 birds and the species has been taken off the Red Data list of endangered birds.

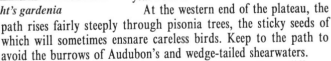

A noddy guarding its egg

From March to November you will see large numbers of lesser noddies and sooty terns. At the peak of the breeding season, the excited cries of the birds make Aride a very noisy place indeed. In addition, Aride has the world's largest colony of lesser noddies and the world's only colony of sooty terns not breeding on a coral island. Roseate terns arrive around the end of April and depart at the end of August. You should know that Aride is their last remaining breeding site in the region.

You may see the Seychelles magpie robin on the coastal plateau, one of the rarest birds in the world. A re-introduction programme is under way on Aride. Aride's unique plants – Wright's gardenia and the newly discovered, night-flowering Aride cucumber – may also be seen. A certain amount of agriculture is also carried out in this area.

Wright's gardenia

Progressing towards the western end of the plateau, you will see ground nesting white-tailed tropicbirds and fairy terns which precariously balance a single egg on a bare tree branch while waiting for it to hatch. Both species breed all year round.

At the western end of the plateau, the path rises fairly steeply through pisonia trees, the sticky seeds of which will sometimes ensnare careless birds. Keep to the path to avoid the burrows of Audubon's and wedge-tailed shearwaters.

The climb to the **Viewing Point** over Aride's northern cliffs can be tiring, especially when it is still and humid, but the view from the summit makes it all worthwhile. Here, you will see hundreds of giant primitive frigatebirds. Two species, great and lesser, roost here, though the nearest breeding site is Aldabra, 1,200km (750 miles) away. With a bit of luck you may also see hawksbill turtles in the turquoise waters below, or catch a glimpse of a red-tailed tropicbird, which has its only breeding site in the region on Aride.

You are taken back to the Visitor's Shelter by the same route, in time for a simple barbecue lunch provided by your boat crew. You may swim or snorkel from the beach, though you should take care when the sea is rough that you do not get swept onto the bare coral outcrops. It is also unsafe to swim near the edges of the island where the currents can be strong. If in any doubt, consult the warden. The reef off Aride is spectacular and well worth seeing if conditions are favourable.

9. Cousin

This is a nature reserve, purchased by rsnc in 1968 following a worldwide campaign, and managed by BirdLife International (International Council for Bird Preservation). Cousin (28ha/69 acres) is second in importance as a seabird island only to Aride, with seven breeding species. There are rare land birds and important nesting beaches for hawksbill turtles. This is a half-day trip.

Roosting fairy terns

– Trips to Cousin are easily arranged through hotels or travel agents on Praslin. Landing is generally possible all year around. The cost of your excursion includes a landing fee payable to BirdLife International –

On arrival, your boat will anchor close to the island where you will transfer onto the the island's boat and land on a sandy beach. From here you will be guided to the boat shed. Tours are given in English and French and you are not allowed to wander at will. Dress in shorts or swimwear and T-shirt and take a plastic bag to protect valuables, cameras and film when landing and leaving, as well as sun cream and a towel. Remember that flash photography is not permitted on the island.

Along the coastal plateau you will see many introduced plants such as cotton, pawpaw and castor oil – remnants of the days when the island was run as a plantation. You will also see indigenous trees such as the tortoise tree, so-called because the smelly fruits resemble the shell of a tortoise. The fruits are also eaten by giant land tortoises, a few of which can be seen on the island.

In this area you will also see Seychelles warblers, the species which – due to the threat of imminent extinction – inspired a worldwide campaign to raise the £15,000 needed to buy the island. The campaign raised about a third of this sum, Cadbury's Chocolates donated another third, and Christopher Cadbury personally gave the final sum needed to save the warbler and the island.

Other land birds in this area are the Seychelles fody – found only here and on Cousine and Frégate islands – and the Malagasy turtle dove. Breeding sea birds include the lesser noddy during the southeast monsoon and fairy tern all year round. Other creatures include

Hawksbill turtle

numerous lizards, giant millipedes and especially the Seychelles skink and Wright's skink.

A short, easy walk uphill leads to the summit of the island at 69m (225ft) above sea level. This affords views towards neighbouring Cousine Island.

Return to the beach; if you are lucky you may encounter a hawksbill turtle, mainly during the months of October–March. Do not approach a turtle coming up the beach in case you scare it back into the sea. Once it has started to lay, it becomes almost oblivious to your presence.

10. Curieuse and St Pierre

Visit Curieuse, former leper colony and home to many giant land tortoises. Take a board walk through the mangrove swamp; then visit the coral reefs of St Pierre to see one of the best snorkelling spots in the granite islands.

– If you also decide to visit Cousin as a morning trip, you can proceed from there to Curieuse and St Pierre for the afternoon. These three combined make an excellent full-day trip. If you decide to do just this trip as a half day on its own, we recommend that you hire a small boat for the morning to avoid the much busier afternoons when other boats arrive. Many small boats are available to take you across to Curieuse. Ask at your hotel reception or one of the tour agents for details –

A trip to Cousin, Curieuse and St Pierre will usually include a Creole barbecue at Curieuse. The food is good but fairly basic with soft drinks provided.

You land on **Curieuse** at **Anse St José**, facing Praslin. You will notice the abandoned plantation house, known as the **Doctor's House** which dominates the shady barbecue site. A short walk away at the western end of the beach are ruins of houses that once belonged to a former leper colony.

The best walk heads inland from the right-hand side of the Doctor's House. There is another ruined building on the right, just before the path climbs upwards. Follow the path up, then down towards a **board walk** through man-

Board walk through mangroves

Barbecue on Curieuse

groves. Take care on the boards as some are loose; it is best to stick to the centre. Bear right at the walk's T-junction and walk along the wall which crosses **Laraie Bay**. This is an old turtle pond – now abandoned – where turtles were kept live prior to shipment.

From here you can see the hills of Curieuse, which are heavily degraded compared to other Seychelles islands. However, coco de mer palms may be seen, this being the only island other than Praslin where they occur naturally.

Reaching the opposite side, the path winds its way through some strange but natural rock sculptures. Look out for an area where there is a wedge of coral about 3m (10ft) above the high tide mark. Samples from sites such as this have been dated as being about 6,000 years old. Curiously, sea levels in Seychelles have fallen since then, whereas worldwide they have been rising. In Seychelles, the ocean level is 5m (16ft) lower than it is in India while sea levels at Praslin and Curieuse are 1m (3ft) lower than at Mahé. The best possible explanation for this is the change in ocean currents.

A short distance further on, at **Grand Anse**, you reach the **giant land tortoise research centre**.
Here, in pens, you can see tortoises from one to five years old. Many, a lot older and larger are roaming loose, brought here from Aldabra. Return to Anse St José by the same route.

Tortoise project signboard

Now it is time for a refreshing swim. Rejoin your boat to get to **St Pierre**. The corals here have suffered some damage from souvenir hunters but the numbers and variety of fish is amazing and this remains one of the best snorkelling sites in the granite islands. Be content just to look and not touch. You will return to Praslin at about 5pm.

Slumbering giant land tortoises

EXCURSIONS

11. Bird Island

To get a complete picture of Seychelles, you must visit at least one coral island. If time is limited, you should make it this one. A colony of a million sooty terns is present from April–October (the best time to visit). The beaches are pristine and there is excellent swimming and snorkelling, or fishing if you wish. Visitors are always refreshed by the feeling of having escaped from the rat race. It seems that the rest of the world simply disappears.

– A minimum stay of one night at Bird Island Lodge, the only accommodation on the island, is necessary as there is only one flight per day departing Mahé at 10.30am and returning from Bird at 11.15am. Flying time is 30 minutes. Bookings for flights and accommodation can be made through a travel agent, the Bird Island Lodge at Tel: 323322 or the Victoria booking office at Tel: 324925 –

Bird is a flat, coralline island 98km (60 miles) northwest of Mahé. In size it is just 1½km (1 mile) by ½km (¼ mile), taking its name from the enormous sooty tern colony. For bird-watchers, October is the best month, combining the spectacle of the tern colony with the chance of seeing rare migrants. Non-birders can simply enjoy the feeling of remoteness and the wild beauty of the island.

On arrival, you are met by the manager of the Lodge and escorted to your chalet. After settling in, assuming you are on Bird at the same time as the sooty terns, you will probably be drawn to investigate the colony by the noise emanating from it. Walk to the **Restaurant** and up the beach, away from the hotel buildings. After about 200m (220yds), a sign points inland to a **Viewing Platform** from where you can watch the action. Even if you miss the sign, the thousands of birds plying back and forth between the colony and the sea will lead you to the spot.

Sooty tern eggs are considered a great delicacy by the Seychellois, which meant that

The awesome sight of a million sooty terns

Esmeralda, the world's largest tortoise

the Bird Island colony was once heavily exploited. Now it is protected by the island's owners. A small number of eggs are taken from areas peripheral to the main colony for use at the Lodge; and tern eggs sometimes feature on the menu there.

Return to the Lodge and ask at Reception about the last reported whereabouts of the island's most famous resident, **Esmeralda**, one of the three giant land tortoises which roam around Bird. Esmeralda (who is a male, despite the name), tips the scales at a hefty 304kg (670 lbs), making him officially the world's heaviest tortoise. Another reptile, the hawksbill turtle, commonly hauls itself up the beach to lay eggs between October and April. The sight of this endangered creature may be some compensation for missing the tern colony, if you cannot time your visit for that.

All meals, simply prepared using fresh ingredients grown on the island like pawpaw, okra, pumpkin, patole, aubergine and chillies, are included in your stay. There is also a small pig and poultry farm, and fish is never a problem; a fresh supply arrives at the lodge's doorstep every day.

If you stay for a few days, you could enjoy a fishing trip. Just north of Bird, the Seychelles Bank slips away to a tremendous depth. A four-hour trip will take you to fishing grounds where sailfish, dorado, bonito

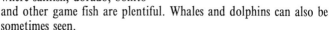
A fiery Bird Island sunset

and other game fish are plentiful. Whales and dolphins can also be sometimes seen.

There is some good snorkelling, and equipment is available from Reception. Ask here for details of the best spots, as conditions change throughout the year and there are sometimes strong currents in certain areas.

Keen bird-watchers should walk to the northern end of the island and check the bushes, scan the the sandbanks for waders and the airstrip – when there are no flights – for passerines. However, the usual thing on Bird is for people to do very little indeed; read a book, swim, wander along the beach looking for shells, watch the sunset, and fall asleep at night listening to the sigh of the sea on the beach. One cannot ask for more.

This is the ultimate get-away-from-it-all island. Desroches is the exposed rim of a submerged atoll, the only island of the Amirantes Group – lying 230km (144 miles) southwest of the granitic islands – to have air links with Mahé. The Desroches Island Lodge is situated at one extremity of the island which is 6km (3½ miles) long and 1km (½ mile) wide. There are stunning beaches, superb diving and other watersports. A minimum stay of two days is necessary.

– There are three flights a week; on Monday, Wednesday and Saturday from the Inter-Island Terminal on Mahé. Bookings for flights and accommodation can be made through a travel agent, the Desroches Island Lodge at Tel: 229003 or the Victoria booking office at Tel:324502. All flights depart 1.10pm and return 2.20pm the same day. Flying time is one hour –

Rustic Desroches Lodge chalets

You will be met by the Desroches Lodge manager on arrival and escorted to the Reception for a welcome drink and check-in. Your booking includes all meals. Lunch is a buffet and dinner may be a candle-lit barbecue – weather permitting – or taken in the restaurant. Naturally, evening entertainment is limited.

Diving is best during October–April when you can explore the **Drop,** an atoll wall. From May–September, diving within the shallow lagoon is possible. The Dive Centre is well-equipped. There are Hobiecats, canoes and water scooters for hire, and you can go paragliding, water skiing or deep sea fishing. Records have been set in Desroches' relatively unfished waters and plaques on the watersports centre testify to this.

The easiest way to explore the island is on a bicycle, which you can borrow from Reception. Avoid the hottest part of the day. The tracks are bumpy and some peter out completely or are blocked by logs. They can also be muddy after heavy rain, so take care. To reach the **Settlement,** cycle or walk – it is within easy walking distance, all on flat land – to the **airstrip** and take the track that is found near the centre of the island and runs

Seychelles lily

Relax on Desroches stunning talcum powder beaches

parallel to the coast, through coconut plantation.

The Settlement is the area where plantation workers have their houses, with a few facilities such as a lock-up, 'hospital' (no equipment, just two rooms with beds), a shop which opens once a week (selling rice, sugar and a few basics) and farm buildings such as the copra drier.

En route to the Settlement, you pass under a forest of coconut palms. Coconuts used to be the mainstay of the island's economy and some copra is still produced. The *kalorifer* at the Settlement is still used though the oil press inland of this, on the opposite side of the path from the coast, is now overgrown. About 40 people work at the Settlement, growing vegetables and tending livestock to supply the Lodge; the surplus is exported to Mahé.

There is little to see beyond the Settlement, apart from an automatic **Lighthouse** at the far end of the island. There is a ladder to the top if you want to get a good view of both sides of the island at once. Just follow the beach or the coastal track down the island to reach it.

Swimming and snorkelling is safe all the way along the inner edge of the lagoon; usually the waters here are like a mill pond, especially during the southeast monsoon from April–September, when the prevailing wind is from the opposite side of the island.

A lone trumpetfish

Desroches is similar in appearance to Bird and has the same sort of Robinson Crusoe atmosphere. The difference is that Desroches is a former plantation and you get to see the remains of a past way of life here.

13. Nature Walks

To reach some of Seychelles' wildest and most atmospheric places, you need to walk. You will see plants and animals found nowhere else on earth and experience the quiet beauty of the forest. Most walks reward with superb views from view-points you will almost certainly have all to yourself.

The Tourism Division has prepared a series of excellent illustrated booklets on sale at their shop in Independence House, Victoria, Mahé. They provide details on the flora, fauna and history you are witnessing and add great pleasure to your experience.

Glacis viewed on the Anse Major walk

The best season for walking is during the cooler, less humid months, especially June to September. The worst time is at the height of the rains, mid-December to January, when paths are muddy and slippery. April is also a difficult month because humidity is high and there is little breeze to cool you down. Avoid the middle of the day for your trek; early morning and late afternoon is best. Remember, it gets dark under the trees by about 6.30pm.

You will need a good pair of shoes for most walks, except for the Danzil-Anse Major walk where ordinary flip flops will do. Walking boots are probably a bit over the top but a decent pair of trainers with a good grip are fine. It is very important to take something to drink, preferably water. You will need a hat, sunglasses and a snack to enjoy when you reach the top, or the end; both are usually the same thing on Seychelles' walks.

Do not overestimate your fitness. Remember, most Seychelles' walks are steep, the paths very uneven and the climate very different for strenuous activity than most of Europe and the US. The humidity, in particular, is very taxing. In the mountains, choose carefully when looking for hand-holds. The endemic palms have spines and tree branches are often rotten and may break off in your hand.

Do not attempt any walk – except perhaps the Danzil-Anse Major path – after rain as the paths will be dangerous.

Danzil-Anse Major Walk: An easy walk along almost the only stretch of Mahé's coast with no road access. It leads to a small secluded beach. There is little shade, so leave early or wait until about 3pm. Keep an eye on your valuables at Anse Major. It would be better for women not to do the walk alone in case you get hassled.

The walk starts at **Auberge Club des Seychelles**, at the end of the road from Beau Vallon to Bel Ombre. You can park where the road widens at the end, just by **Scala Restaurant**, and walk up the hill past the hotel. If you are travelling by bus, the bus stop is just here also. Ask for Scala Restaurant.

Follow the road up the hill; soon it becomes a track and then a well marked path, crossing the Danzil River. Highlights of the walk include wonderful views of Beau Vallon and Silhouette Island, and spectacular areas of granitic rock slopes known as *glacis*. It should take about 1½ hours to reach Anse Major at a leisurely pace. You return by the same route. There are no facilities at Anse Major, so you may wish to take food and drink.

La Reserve and Brulee Walk: This is Mahé's answer to Praslin's Vallée de Mai; the island's best area of palm forest, with five of Seychelles' six unique palm species – only the coco de mer is missing. There are viewpoints over vertical granite cliffs which are sometimes adorned with shy sprays of flowering orchids.

The starting point is reached from Victoria by driving south and taking the **Montagne Posee Road** at Anse aux Pins, just after the old plantation house with the sign 'Lenstiti Kreol'. Close to the summit of this pass is a signboard on the left for Cable and Wireless. Park on the left, just inside the entrance. Do not block the access. The trail begins here, climbing the steep hill to the left under mahogany trees.

It is quite well signposted, but without the detailed booklet there are two points where you may go wrong. First, after you have climbed the short, steep hill, you will come out onto a rocky area. Turn 90 degrees to the left and you will pick up the trail running along the edge of the mahogany plantation (even if you are not a botanist, you can recognise the plantation by the ordered ranks of the trees, in comparison with the general untidiness of wild woodland). The second danger spot is about 150m (164yds) further on, where the trail turns 90 degrees to the right. There is supposed to be a post here with an arrow pointing uphill but it is not obvious if you are not looking for it, and occasionally it falls down.

Footpath and sign for La Reserve

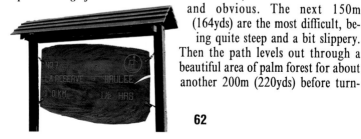

From here, the trail is well marked and obvious. The next 150m (164yds) are the most difficult, being quite steep and a bit slippery. Then the path levels out through a beautiful area of palm forest for about another 200m (220yds) before turning uphill again. On this stretch you have a choice. A sign points to the left, indicating a circular path marked with green spots. We suggest that if you are flagging at this point, you keep straight on, following the yellow spots up the there-and-back path to the viewing point. This overlooks Anse Boileau and the islands of Ile aux Vaches, Thérese and Conception.

To the right of Conception is Morne Blanc, then **Morne Seychellois**, the highest point for a thousand miles around. This walk should take about 1½ hours up and an hour down.

Tea Factory-Morne Blanc Walk: This is a short, sharp climb to the summit of a mountain, which from the west coast looks unassailable. However, the track behind this vertical face is not too difficult and the views are breathtaking. There is some very spooky rainforest at the top, which gives you some idea of what it is like in the high forests of Mahé without committing yourself to an all-day hike.

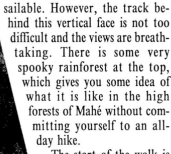

The start of the walk is close to the **Tea Company** on the **Sans Souci** road. From the Tea Company, it is about 200m (220yds) in the direction of Victoria.

Mighty Morne Blanc

The path rises to 250m (820ft) from the road to a height of 667m (2,188ft) above sea level. The walk is within Morne Seychellois National Park and you will see many of Seychelles' unique plants and hear frogs chirping but see surprisingly few birds. You may also see Seychelles wolf snakes and possibly the Seychelles house snake (though this is less likely as they are nocturnal); both are harmless.

From the summit you can see both sides of Mahé at once. The islands of St Anne Marine National Park are to the east and most of the west coast as far as Ansé la Mouche will be in view. Silhouette Island is also visible to the right. Take care at the summit. The cliff you are standing on is almost vertical and it is a long way down. Return via the same route. It should take about an hour to reach the top and about half that to descend; even less if you are careless on the cliff top!

14. Diving

Seychelles is probably one of the best places in the world to learn how to dive. The water is warm and usually clear, the fish friendly, the underwater scenery superb and the facilities excellent. Much of the best diving is to be had on shallow reefs, ideal for beginners. Seychelles offers some challenging and exhilarat-

Huff and pufferfish!

ing dive sites, offering spectacular encounters with rays and whale sharks.

We recommend the **Seychelles Underwater Centre** (Tel: 247357, daily 8.30am–5pm), situated at Coral Strand Hotel, Beau Vallon, Mahé because we both learned to dive here, and having subsequently dived in many places the world over, we have yet to find its equal for standards of safety, equipment and friendliness.

If you are not sure diving is for you, take the one-day introductory course available on weekdays. You should book at least a day ahead. You start at 9.30am with a theory session, followed by a session in the swimming pool to familiarise yourself with the equipment. A break for lunch and then it's a boat dive in the afternoon, accompanied by an instructor. You return to Mahé at 3.30pm. There is no certificate issued but it does give you a good idea of what diving is all about.

If you do decide to take the plunge, you will spend four days obtaining a PADI Open Water Certificate, which will then enable you to hire equipment and dive worldwide. These courses are available on request and run every week. There are five theory sessions, five pool sessions and four sea dives. The price of the course includes a diving manual, full equipment rental and all dives. Courses are run in English, French and German. Other more advanced PADI courses are also available.

Having learned to dive, you can really explore the wonders of the coral reef. The reefs around the granite islands are pretty rather than spectacular, in comparison with the Red Sea for example, but the numbers and variety of fish species is tremendous. Seychelles Underwater Centre runs trips to 30 inshore sites (6–25m depth) and 12 offshore sites (15–30m depth) for certified divers. Live aboard charters to more remote destinations can be arranged by the centre.

15. Watersports

The same good reasons apply for enjoying watersports in Seychelles as for diving. The weather is good, the sea is warm and inviting and there are excellent facilities available.

The best equipment and widest range of activities are offered on **Beau Vallon** beach on **Mahé**, but most large hotels and island lodges carry some equipment.

Leisure 2000 (no telephone) of Beau Vallon are the only APA (American Paragliding Association) internationally qualified paragliding operation in Seychelles. Situated next to Coral Strand Hotel, they have discounted rates for

Paraglider at Beau Vallon

hotel residents and those staying at Auberge Club des Seychelles, Fisherman's Cove, Sunset Beach and Vista Bay Club.

There are no motorized watersports available before noon on weekdays, so as not to interfere with the nets of the mackerel fishermen. Apart from this restriction, Leisure 2000 is open daily (10am–5pm) except 1 January. Motorized sports on offer after the restricted hours are water skiing and water scooters. Hobiecats, windsurfers, canoes and bellyboards can be hired by the hour and snorkelling equipment by the day. For novices, Hobiecat, windsurfing and skiing lessons are available from Leisure 2000.

Beau Vallon is not always the best place to play in the sea. It is quite sheltered during May–October. There is no point hiring a windsurfer if the sea is like a mill pond. By the same token, you may think twice about paragliding in unsettled weather.

16. Deep Sea Fishing

Seychelles offers excellent opportunities for big game fishing. Possible catches include sailfish, kingfish, shark, dorado, bonito, and occasionally marlin, depending on the season. You can fish all year round, although unsettled weather during the peak of the rainy season (mid-December to end of January), can cause cancellations on occasion.

If you are staying in the Beau Vallon area, we recommend the Mancienne brothers whose

Fishing around

shop, The Boat House (Tel: 247898), is situated north of the Coral Strand Hotel where the coast road turns inland towards Victoria. It is best to call at the shop (open daily 8.30am–6pm) and discuss your plans. Special programmes can be arranged to suit you personally and can include trips to other islands and snorkelling. Departure and return times are flexible.

Richard Mancienne operates three different boats: *Blue Marlin*, *Albatross* and *Yellowfin*. In *Blue Marlin* and *Albatross* you can have eight rods out simultaneously, and carry a recommended maximum of six people, although they can take 10. *Yellowfin* carries a maximum of 16 persons, and again can have up to eight rods out at once. This boat is faster and capable of going further afield.

Fishing trips can be arranged any day, subject to availability. Lunch and soft drinks are included in the price together with island landing fees, if applicable. Trips usually depart at 9am and return in the evening at 6pm. Fishing is best up to noon and then from 3pm onwards, so an island visit for lunch makes a good break at a time when there is little action. August–December is best for sailfish, January–March for kingfish (or wahoo), November–December for *karang* (or trevally). Tuna, bonito and dorado may be caught all year around.

Night fishing trips – the price includes snacks and soft drinks – may also be arranged, departing at 5pm and returning around midnight. You can go bottom fishing for red snapper, known locally as *bourzwa*, and green jobfish or *zob*. You can choose to bring your catch on board or cast it back to fight another day. On return to Beau Vallon, you may keep all or some of your catch as you wish. No fish will be wasted, you can be sure.

No previous experience is necessary and the friendly, helpful boatmen are happy to give instruction for no extra charge. The boats carry safety equipment, first aid kits and a radio link. If you arrange to have snorkelling included in your trip, this equipment can also be included.

Caught unawares

Warlord, based at Anse Royale during the northwest monsoon and Anse a la Mouche in the southeast is ultra fast, capable of reaching Praslin in 45 minutes. She carries a maximum of eight people and fishes with six rods simultaneously. *Warlord*'s speed is its greatest asset. It specialises in fishing from The Drop, where the Seychelles Bank drops away to great depths and the big fish lurk. The boat covers the 37 nautical miles in just 70 minutes. Half-day trips leave around 7–7.30am, returning four hours later, or leave at 1pm, returning at 5pm. Full-day trips, with or without an island visit, are also available and the price will include lunch and as many drinks as you want.

If you are based in south Mahé, bookings for *Warlord* can be made through Francois Jackson (Tel: 376458). Other game fishing boats, based in Port Victoria, are available through Marine Charter Association (Tel: 332126).

17. Cruising

If you have the time and money, this can be the experience of a lifetime. You will see some of the world's most remote and beautiful islands, many of which are uninhabited. Cruising arrangements should be made well in advance. There are several liveaboard charter boats – which include diving – based in Seychelles.

Bookings can be made through local travel agents or directly with owners.

Two of the most well established and reliable outfits are Captain Bob Brown (Brownie), and Michel Gardet. Brownie (PO Box 504, Victoria, Mahé, Tel: 224573), has a 21-m (70-ft) motor cruiser called *My Way*, equipped with all the necessary modern equipment, compressor and full dive equipment. Eight persons can be accommodated. Brownie is one of the most experienced skippers in the waters around Seychelles.

Michel Gardet (Aqua Diving (Pty) Ltd, Villas de Mer, Amitie, Praslin, Tel: 233015) also has great experience and knowledge of the outer islands. He has a motor/sail catamaran, *King Bambo*, fully fitted with a compressor and full dive equipment. Six persons can be accommodated for long trips.

The best time for cruising is mid-September to mid-December. Thereafter until March, there can be unsettled weather and a risk of cyclones in the southern islands. April to May is also good while from June to mid-September, the southeast monsoon brings rough seas which are uncomfortable for long passages. It really is essential to book well in advance if you want to go as far afield as **Aldabra**, located 400km (250 miles) from Mahé. Shorter trips can usually be arranged with less notice.

Allow a minimum of five days for a trip to the **Amirantes**, a group of islands approximately 200km (125 miles) west of Mahé, an extra two days to get to the **Alphonse** group with its superb diving, and 14 days minimum for a return trip to the Aldabra group (although 21 days would be better). Aldabra Atoll, the world's largest raised atoll is the Holy Grail for the cruising fraternity. Attractions include the world's largest population of giant land tortoises – 150,000, or about five times more than the Galapagos – and the last remaining flightless bird of the Indian Ocean, the white-throated rail.

Cruise yacht leaving Victoria

Shopping

There is very little in the way of traditional handicrafts or gifts that are special to Seychelles. The souvenir industry is a fairly recent phenomenon which has sprung up in response to the growth in tourism. It is worth having a good look around and visiting many of the artisans themselves before deciding what to buy. Prices are usually fixed and generally high, though some street traders may load their prices in response to tourist expectations that they should bargain. In shops, you should not expect any bargaining. The products listed below are found almost exclusively on Mahé, with the exception of the coco de mer nuts. Shopping in Praslin is expensive and the range of items is small. Shopping is very limited on the other islands.

A splash of local colour

What to Buy

Batiks

Ron Gerlach uses this Indonesian technique to produce a product that is uniquely Seychellois. His studio (Monday–Friday 10am–12.30pm, 1.30–5pm, Saturday 10am–12.30pm, closed Sunday), is on Beau Vallon beach, halfway between the Coral Strand Hotel and the Baobab Pizzeria. Gerlach is President of the Nature Protection Trust of Seychelles.

Ron Gerlach sun-drying bati

Boxes

Guy Ceasar produces beautiful boxes inlaid with local woods and mother of pearl. He recycles old furniture for the inlays, so no rare trees are felled. The boxes are polished using wax and oiled with cinnamon. Ceasar's boxes are on sale at **Antigone Trading**, Victoria Arcade – near Temooljees department store – and in other shops.

Art

Several artists are mentioned in the Mahé *Day 1 Itinerary*. Another artist well worth visiting is **Vladimir**; his studio at Glacis is – coming from Beau Vallon – just after Northolme Hotel. His colourful signpost is unmistakable. The work of **Egbert Marday**, on sale at CODEVAR (Albert Street, Victoria, Mahé) is also very good.

Pottery

In addition to shops and studios mentioned in the Mahé *Day 1 Itinerary*, visit CODEVAR which sells some attractive and unusual pottery items.

Woven Crafts and Mats

Woven table mats, hats and baskets are inexpensive. CODEVAR and other shops have a good selection. You can try the **stalls** by the **Clock Tower** in Victoria for hats.

Mats printed with some very beautiful photographs of Seychelles may be purchased from **Photo Eden**, Independence Avenue, Victoria. Photo Eden also carries a variety of other gifts, such as large photograph albums with a map of Mahé embossed on the covers.

Some people like to take home the local grass brushes, the *zig* and the *fatak*. Locally made ones are usually on sale on the edges of the market on Saturday mornings.

Tea and Spices

Seychelles Tea Company sell packs of teas with vanilla, lemon, orange and cinnamon flavours. A packet with all the ingredients you need to make a real Seychelles curry, including cinnamon bark, the *kari pile* and other spices, can be bought at **Victoria market** (especially the stalls to the right of the entrance from Market Street). Here, you can sometimes also buy a coconut stool, with a sharp spike attached at one end for grating coconuts. There are also dried vanilla pods for sale.

The appropriately named 'Hellfire' on sale at the market is pickled hot chillies. This is something that we find ourselves constantly taking home for friends who miss their 'real' chilli sauce dearly.

Lorna Reeve's hand-painted jewellery

Perfumes

Kreol Fleurage Parfums of North East Point, Mahé (Tel: 241329), produces three perfumes using no fewer than 102 local plants, 35 percent of which have never previously been used for perfumes. The perfumes are also on sale in many hotel and souvenir shops, not to mention Harrods in London.

Model Boats

They can be found in CODEVAR on Mahé, and at **Sunset Beach Hotel**; also check out at the workshops of **La Marine** and **Souverains des Mers** (see Mahé *Day 1 Itinerary*).

Jewellery

Lorna Reeves produces jewellery by hand-painting sea polished glass and basalt, a truly unique and environmentally friendly souvenir. On sale at CODEVAR.

Coco de Mer

The best place to buy a whole coco de mer is the **Forestry Station**, Fond B'Offay, Praslin (Monday–Friday 8am–4pm). They are also available in almost every tourist shop, polished and unpolished. You must make sure that the vendor gives you an export certificate to go with the nut, or you will have problems with customs. Remember that the little ones are not genuine; they are made out of wood. Some nuts have been hollowed out so that they are lighter for carriage, and unless you want a door stop, it is probably best to buy one of these. You will also see items such as fruit bowls or vases made out of coco de mer.

Going nutty

Clothing

If you look carefully, you will find items which are genuinely locally produced, ie, the fabric is printed and sewn in Seychelles. **Sunstroke Boutique** in Market Street and at Beau Vallon – near the Police Station – carries a wide range of T-shirts, beachwear, shorts, dresses etc, many of which are very original. There are T-shirts everywhere but **Oceana** at Oceangate House has a good range, including some tiny ones for little children. Oceana also stocks a range of gossamer-thin, cool lounge wear such as tie-dyed kaftans, as well as dresses and trousers. **Brijals**, Jivan Building, Church Street, will reproduce your holiday snap or whatever you like on a T-shirt.

A riot of casual beachwear

Monthly Craft Market

It is unlikely you will plan your entire holiday around the monthly craft market but if you are here at the right time, you should call in. It is organized and held, usually on the last weekend of each month, at CODEVAR. The craft market is open from 9am–5.30pm and artists and craftsmen from all over Seychelles come to set up stalls to display and sell their work, and will be happy to chat with visitors about what they do.

You can have your portrait sketched while you wait or listen to the Creole bands which perform throughout the day. The timing of the craft fair does vary at times, in order to coincide with cruise-ship visits.

What Not To Buy

You will see tortoiseshell on sale almost everywhere, made from the polished shell of the endangered hawksbill turtle. The animal is killed to obtain this and the meat discarded because it can sometimes cause poisoning if eaten. All marine turtles are listed as endangered by the Convention on International Trade in Endangered Species, which Seychelles signed on 26 January 1977. This means that all international trade in tortoiseshell is banned. It is illegal to import the product into most countries of the world, including Europe and the US.

Corals, coral jewellery and shells all look very attractive displayed on the stalls but once again, what you are actually looking at are rows of dead bodies. Local reefs remain attractive and relatively unexploited because tourism is quite a new phenomena here, but if the demand for coral and shells is sustained or begins to grow, the reefs here will be decimated as they have been in so many other places. Seychelles is a middle income country and it does not need to sacrifice its natural assets and beauty to ensure the daily survival of its people.

Eating Out

Local fish is excelle...

The Seychellois are among the world's greatest per capita consumers of fish. The reason for this one-food obsession is its availability and quality. The fish in Seychelles is really more flavourful than those found in other waters. Amongst the best tasting fish is red snapper (*bourzwa*) – although the French spelling, *bourgeois*, is often used on menus. The white-fleshed Job – Creole *zob* – is also very tasty. Steaks from larger fish are also nearly always available, in particular tuna. Those who have never had a tuna steak are often surprised by just how meaty it is in taste and texture. Other excellent fish steaks come from kingfish – the local name for what Americans call wahoo, and *karang* – known elsewhere as trevally – and usually on the menu under the French spelling, *carangue*.

Surprisingly, apart from fish, there is not a great deal of local seafood around for a mid-ocean country. Lobster is almost always imported as local stocks have been over-fished. Crabs are in fairly plentiful supply and recently, local prawns have appeared in shops and restaurants following the establishment of a prawn farm on Coetivy Island.

There are just two species of shellfish used regularly in cooking. One is the *tektek*, a small burrowing shellfish found on sandy beaches and the other, which looks like a small clam, is the *palourd*. *Tektek* is always served in soup, stewed with onions, garlic, ginger and parsley. *Palourd*, most often served soaking in aromatic garlic butter, is a great starter.

Octopus in Seychelles is superb. If you have tried it elsewhere and dismissed it as chewy and rubbery, give it another chance in Seychelles. It makes a delicious starter in octopus salad or as a main course in a curry cooked with coconut milk. Either way, it will

A Seychellois housewife cooking up a storm

melt in your mouth. The bad news is that it has been exploited heavily because it is so good, and catches are falling steadily.

If you are trying out the local cuisine, there should be a little dish of chilli sauce somewhere on the table. Take it easy until you've sampled a little, even if

A no-holds-barred champagne brunch

you like hot food. The tiny Seychelles chillies are like dynamite. Likewise, local curries are quite hot, but we find them delicious and full of flavour.

Nearly all restaurants offer at least some meat or chicken dishes too. Make the most of the main courses and starters, because unless you are thrilled to bits by fresh tropical fruits – mango, pawpaw, banana, passionfruit, guava and so on – Seychelles deserts are often disappointing. The choice is usually ice cream or fruit salad.

Drinks

After dinner, you could try *citronelle* tea instead of normal tea or coffee. This is made by pouring boiling water onto lemon grass, a common but wonderfully fragrant grass found in the mountains. This refreshing infusion is also supposed to help digestion.

The locally brewed lager beers, Seybrew and Eku, are excellent. There is a range of fizzy soft drinks available from Seybrew and other manufacturers, including bitter lemon, orangeade, ginger ale, tonic and soda water. Just make sure that you ask for 'Sport' not lemonade. It is always worth asking if there is any fresh lime available. This drink of freshly squeezed limes with water and a hint of sugar or salt – according to your preference – is really refreshing but very rarely on offer. Most hotels and restaurants serve fruit juices from tins or packets, although a few are now offering freshly squeezed juices. Bear in mind that wines are all imported and are very expensive when eating out.

Recommendations

The restaurants highlighted in the preceding itineraries and on the following pages represent the best of eating out in Seychelles. The

following price categories are for a three-course meal for one person, excluding drinks and service charge: Expensive = SR250 and above, Moderate = SR150–SR250, Inexpensive = SR150 and below.

A Creole buffet featuring fish and fresh coconut

The famed Marie Antoinette

ETOILE DE MER
Anse Etoile, Mahé
Tel: 241327
Situated on the northeast coast, north of Victoria. International and imaginative Creole cuisine. Restaurant has a friendly atmosphere and service is good. Open lunch and dinner except Monday. *Moderate.*

Mahé

MARIE ANTOINETTE
Grand Trianon, St Louis, Mahé
Tel: 266222
The easiest place to try traditional Creole food. Marie Antoinette is situated on the hill overlooking Victoria – on the road over to Beau Vallon – and housed in a beautiful old colonial dwelling. The decor inside is simple but attractive. The menu is fixed with a starter – probably *tektek* soup – five small main courses, four of which are fish dishes, usually including parrot fish, tuna and *bourzwa*, and a simple dessert of fruit salad. Open every day except Sunday for lunch and dinner. It can get quite busy. *Inexpensive.*

DANIELLE'S
Vista Bay Club, Glacis, Mahé
Tel: 247914
This restaurant, which is part of the small hotel but open to non-residents, has a wonderful location; built on a sort of deck over the rocks of the Glacis coast. The sea below is floodlit at night. Sadly, its spectacular site means it is vulnerable to strong winds and heavy rain, and diners may have to move indoors if the weather is inclement. Wise to check the weather before you go. The service is good, with International and Creole cuisine. Open daily, evenings only. *Moderate.*

LA MARIE GALANTE
Grand Anse, Mahé
Tel: 378455
Another beautiful spot to have a meal, so perhaps it should be lunch you try here in order to enjoy the view. The chef really puts his heart into the cooking and comes up with imaginative dishes, as well as doing the usual dishes very well. Open for lunch and dinner every day except Monday. *Moderate to Expensive.*

View from Marie Galante Restaurant

Upmarket Scala Restaurant

SCALA RESTAURANT
Bel Ombre, Mahé
Tel: 247535
Italian, international and sophisticated Creole cuisine. Excellent food and service. Make reservations, particularly at weekends. Open evenings only. Closed Sunday. *Expensive.*

Oven at Baobab Pizzeria

CHEZ BAPTISTA
Takamaka, Mahé
No Telephone
Simple, well-cooked food. Very fresh fish is the speciality. Creole cuisine in a rustic setting. *Inexpensive.*

L'ISLETTE
L'Islette Island, off Port Glaud, Mahé
Tel: 378229
Mostly Creole cuisine. It is fun to eat here, just for the novelty of being on such a tiny island — the restaurant covers most of it. To get there, drive to Port Glaud and park by the beach opposite the church. Then, simply hail the boat over to ferry you across a short stretch of water. Open daily for lunch and dinner. *Inexpensive.*

LA PERLE NOIRE
Beau Vallon, Mahé
Tel: 247046
International and sophisticated Creole cuisine. Excellent food and service. If you are fed up of fish, come here for a superb steak. If you are not fed up of fish, then they have some wonderful fish dishes too. Open daily, lunch and dinner. *Expensive.*

BAOBAB PIZZERIA
Beau Vallon, Mahé
Tel: 247167
Good pizzas and Italian pasta dishes right on the beach — you eat with your feet in the sand. A relaxed atmosphere. *Inexpensive.*

Praslin

LES ROCHERS
La Pointe, Praslin
Tel: 233034
Located on the coast between Baie St Anne and Grand Anse, the views over what is probably the most beautiful coast on the island are superb. This is certainly the most sophisticated restaurant on Praslin, and many say it is the best in Seychelles. International and Creole cuisine. Open lunch time only. Closed Sunday. *Expensive.*

BLACK PARROT RESTAURANT
Anse Cimitiére, Praslin
Tel: 233900
A good choice of local and international cuisine. The restaurant belongs to the neighbouring Coco de Mer Hotel at Anse Bois de Rose but is open to all. Open for lunch and dinner. *Moderate.*

THE WORLD FAMOUS
La Perle Noire
Restaurant
◄◄ 150 YARDS AHEAD ◄◄

LAURIER RESTAURANT
Anse Volbert, Praslin
Tel: 232241
Unpretentious restaurant serving Creole food. Located next to the Praslin Beach Hotel. Open for lunch and dinner, closed Sunday. *Moderate.*

Nightlife

Visitors do not come to Seychelles for the nightlife. After a day of sun and sand, all but the most dedicated are too worn out for discos. Most tourists who come here have chosen Seychelles because it *is* unsophisticated in such respects. However, the larger hotels in Mahé do have bands a few nights a week and often have their own discotheques. Sometimes, there are displays of local dances, like the *sega* or other activities such as limbo dancing – which seems to have nothing whatsoever to do with Seychelles at all. Smaller hotels and restaurants sometimes have a lone singer-guitarist who sings about coco de mer nuts and laments about going back to the Seychelles.

Night owls should not entirely despair, however. There is no need to resort to tramping up and down the beach all night with your Walkman turned up loud. There are a few good discotheques, two casinos and a cinema in Mahé.

The best recommendation we can make for Praslin is an early night! The only nightlife provided by hotels, like a band or the odd disco, will be limited and irregular. Most people will not want to venture far at night on poor roads with no lighting, so any amusement you find has to be within walking distance.

Locals whooping it up

Nightclubs

LOVENUT
Revolution Avenue, Victoria, Mahé
Tel: 323232
Open weekends only 9pm–3am. Kara-oke nights. Happy Hours last until 11pm.

KATIOLO CLUB
Anse Faure, Mahé
Tel: 375453
Colourful Creole-style nightclub. Friday night is Ladies Night till 11pm. On Saturday, there may be a buffet dinner followed by an open-air disco, weather permitting, until 3am.

FLAMBOYANT
Bois de Rose Avenue, Victoria, Mahé
Tel: 224030
The disco is open Fridays and Saturdays 9pm–3am.

TWILIGHT
Le Surmer Hotel, Point Conan, Mahé
Tel: 241811
Disco every Friday and Saturday until late. Restaurant facilities.

The unpretentious Twilight disco

Casinos

CASINO DES SEYCHELLES
Beau Vallon Bay Hotel,
Beau Vallon, Mahé
Tel: 247272
Gaming tables are open 7pm–3am, slot machines from 10am. Free transport to the casino can be arranged from most of the hotels. A relaxed and friendly atmosphere for amateur gamblers prevails. Dress up if you want to, but it isn't essential.

PLANTER'S CASINO
Plantation Club, PO Box 437,
Baie Lazare, Mahé
Tel: 361361
Planter's is considerably more chic than Casino des Seychelles. It gaming tables are open from 8pm–2am, slot machines from 10am–2am. Again, free transport can be arranged from Equator, Mahé Beach and Barbarons hotels.

Cinema

DEEPAMS CINEMA
Albert Street, Victoria, Mahé
Tel: 322585
Deepams Cinema is not the most luxurious cinema in the world but if it's the film you are interested in, that is all that matters. Obviously, the films here are not the latest releases, but Seychelles is not that far behind. You may well find you have an opportunity to catch up on a particular film that you missed when it was first released and which has not yet been released on video tape.

Calendar of Special Events

Until the advent of tourism, there were no special events in Seychelles for which visitors would time their holidays; the only exception being the usual Catholic festivals, some of which involve modest parades. Public holidays are mainly religious or political, and celebrations are low-key. The town is not even illuminated or dressed up much for Christmas and New Year. However, a few events have started in recent years which do attract tourists in addition to the locals, and some could merit a special consideration for the tourist. As some dates vary from year to year, check with the respective organisations or the Seychelles Tourism Division in Victoria, Mahé.

Festival happenings

APRIL/MAY

Fishing Competitions: The National Fishing Competition, organized by the Rotary Club of Victoria, PO Box 395, Victoria (Tel: 224206), is held in April each year. Other competitions are held from time to time by the Marine Charter Association, PO Box 469, Victoria (Tel: 322126). It is advisable to charter a boat well in advance if you wish to participate. Fishing is a subject dear to the Seychellois soul, and all boats are soon filled during this period.

Festival of Underwater Images: The big event of the year for divers is SUBIOS, the Indian Ocean Festival of Underwater Images, held in the last week of April or first week in May each year. Entertainment, centred around the hotels of Beau Vallon, includes underwater films and talks by world experts. There is an underwater photography contest with prizes, usually donated by local companies. Dive centres run inshore and long range dives for the participants. Further details can be obtained from travel agents, the Ministry of Tourism, Independence House, Victoria (Tel: 225313), or the Seychelles Underwater Centre, Beau Vallon (Tel: 247357).

SEPTEMBER

Beau Vallon Regatta: It is doubtful that you would fly several thousand miles to see it, but there is a two-day regatta held annually at Beau Vallon on the last weekend of September. Depending on your tastes, you might see this as a definite plus, or a big minus if you are staying at one of the Beau Vallon hotels, so it is worth bearing in mind when you choose your holiday dates. The regatta is organized by the Seychelles Round Table and includes a yacht race, swimming competition and other fun competitions such as an underwater treasure hunt, beach tug-of-war and eating and drinking contests.

Evening entertainment may include live music, a fashion show and perhaps a magic show. There are stalls selling food and drink, including beer, and other stalls with simple games typical of any fair. For more details, contact the Round Table Mahé.

Tourism Week: This event takes place in the last week in September. There are bands, *moutya* evenings, cultural evenings, and various events of local colour at the hotels.

OCTOBER

Creole Festival: The biggest cultural event of the year is the Creole Festival, held in the last week of October. Created by the Bannzil Kreol Association in 1985, this is an international gathering of Creole artists from countries with a similar cultural background to Seychelles, including Mauritius and the Caribbean. The capital city of Victoria is decorated with colourful posters and other more offbeat items – in 1992 it was gaily-painted totem poles. There are dances, concerts, plays and processions to entertain the crowds.

A great deal of it has little to do with Seychelles' cultural heritage in particular, but the festival is helping to mould a sense of national identity in a young country; together with an awareness of how Seychelles fits in with the rest of the world.

More details can be obtained from the Creole Festival Committee, Ministry of Education, Mont Fleuri, Mahé (Tel: 225477).

Practical Information

GETTING THERE

By Air

Unless you arrive by cruiseship, you will fly to Seychelles and land at Seychelles International Airport, built on reclaimed land at Pointe Larue on the eastern coast of Mahé.

Air Seychelles has two flights a week from London via Frankfurt or Zurich and once a week each from Madrid, Paris and Rome. It also flies once a week to and from Singapore. Connections to the US are via Singapore or the European hubs. British Airways has two flights a

week from London. Direct flights take nine hours; flights with one stop take 12 hours. Air France has three flights a week from Paris. Condor operates one non-stop flight a week from Frankfurt while Aeroflot fly once a week from Moscow.

Air Seychelles has a weekly service from Johannesburg with a flight time of 4½ hours. Kenya Airways has two flights a week, non-stop from Nairobi.

The cheapest direct flights are usually with Air Seychelles. Good deals on flights are sometimes available with Kenya Airways, changing at Nairobi. Rock-bottom fares are available on Aeroflot, if travelling time is no object: the trip involves an overnight stay in Moscow, then a

Upmarket cruising on the Renaissance

flight from Moscow via Larnaca, Aden and Dar-es-Salaam.

By Sea

Cruiseship companies that specialise in trips to Seychelles include **Noble Caledonia Ltd**, London (UK Tel: 071-491-4752) and **Starline Cruises Ltd**, Mombasa (Kenya Tel: 254-11-485220). There is one cruiseship based in Seychelles, *Renaissance Eight*, operated by **Renaissance Cruises Inc**, Fort Lauderdale (USA Tel: (1) 305-4630982). **Fantasea Cruises** (USA Tel: (1) 310-3928054) operate a luxury motor cruiser specialising in diving, eco-yachting and executive charters. The Seychelles agent for all these companies is **Mahé Shipping Co Ltd**, Shipping House, PO Box 336, Victoria (Tel: 322100).

TRAVEL ESSENTIALS

When to Visit

Any time of year, although the rainiest period of mid-December to end of January is best avoided. Some hotels also charge a supplement during this peak period and again during Easter and August, coinciding with holidays in Europe.

The nicest times are during the calmer months between the two monsoons; April–May or October–November. Calm seas make for pleasant crossings and excellent visibility for snorkellers and divers.

pril–May is a good time for bird watch-
rs to catch the beginning of the breeding
eason for most seabirds. October is the
est month for seeing migrant birds.

July–September is also very pleasant,
hough strong winds make some beaches
ifficult or dangerous for swimming and
ea passages bumpy.

Visas and Passports

ou will need a valid international pass-
ort. Visas are not required by any na-
ionality. Driving licences issued by any
ational body are accepted; an Inter-
ational Driving Permit is not necessary.

Vaccinations

o vaccinations are essential, although
ome doctors recommend polio and ty-
hoid shots. There is no malaria, yellow
ever or other fearsome tropical diseases
n Seychelles.

Customs

isitors are permitted 2 litres of wine or
pirits, 200 cigarettes or 50 cigars and a
mall bottle of perfume. Video tapes must
e declared and may be retained for secu-
ity screening. Firearms – including spear
uns – fruit and animal products are
anned.

Weather

here is no winter, spring or autumn in
eychelles. It is summer all year round,
with temperatures varying little from one
month to the next in the range 24–30°C.

What does vary considerably is the humidity and rainfall. The islands are so
green and attractive because rainfall is
igh, particularly during the northwest

monsoon, from November–April, reaching a peak from mid-December to the end
of January. Heavy showers are possible at
any time of year. Humidity is highest in
April, in the lull before the start of the
southeast monsoon from May–October.
Humidity is lowest during the southeast
monsoon. The mountains are generally
cooler with far higher rainfall. Mahé and
Silhouette have the highest rainfall levels
because they are more mountainous than
the others.

Clothing

Sunglasses, shorts, T-shirts and flip flops
are standard. A sun hat is useful. Do not
wander around town or board buses and
taxis in swimwear or without a top. The
Seychellois take offence. Warm clothing
is not needed except at sea at night.

Some hotels require men to wear long
trousers in public areas after 7.30pm. A
jacket and tie are not required, even for
businessmen, unless you are joining a
cruiseship. Ladies do not need sophisticated evening gowns; simple, cool cotton
dresses will do.

Life's a beach

Electricity

Seychelles' electrical current is 240 volts
AC. Sockets are three point (square pin),
the same as in UK. A torch can be useful
as power cuts are fairly frequent.

Time Differences

Seychelles time is four hours ahead of
Greenwich Mean Time (GMT).

GETTING ACQUAINTED

Geography

Seychelles consists of 115 islands with a
total land mass of 453sq km (175sq miles).
They are spread over an Exclusive Econo-

Perpetual summer and sunny skies

mic Zone of 1,340,000sq km (517,400 sq miles).

The main islands, where 99 percent of Seychellois live, are the world's only granitic outcrops in mid-ocean, all other ocean islands being either volcanic or coralline in origin. Their origin can be traced back to the super-continent of

Granite outcrops at Curieuse

Pangaea which encompassed all the world's continents 200 million years ago. Pangaea broke up, forming Laurasia to the north – modern North America, Europe and Asia, and Gondwanaland – the southern continents – to the south. India, wedged between Madagascar and Africa on one side and Antarctica to the other, broke off and drifted across what was the Sea of Tethys, now the Indian Ocean. Seychelles broke away from the western edge of India close to the Deccan Plateau, and was thus isolated.

In addition, there are many coral islands. Closest to the granitic group are Bird and Denis, both of which can be reached by air from Mahé. They are sand cays, with no barrier reef.

South of Mahé lie Platte and Coetivy, two isolated coral islands. Approximately 200km (125 miles) west of Mahé is the Amirantes chain – an arc of coral platform islands and atolls covering an area of ocean approximately 180km (113 miles) by 35km (22 miles). Beyond the Amirantes is the Farquhar Group. Farquhar is the largest atoll in Seychelles

and lies much closer to Madagascar than to Mahé.

Further west again, to the extreme southwestern corner of Seychelles' Exclusive Economic Zone, is the Aldabra group of islands. These are raised limestone platform islands and atolls, up to 8m (26ft) above sea level. This rare type of island was formed when sea levels fell a few thousand years ago due to a change in ocean currents within the Indian Ocean.

Two islands, Silhouette and North, are of volcanic origin.

Economy

Today, the principal source of foreign exchange receipts is tourism. Fishing, especially tuna fishing, is vital to the economy. Much tuna is canned locally for export.

Religion

The vast majority of Seychellois are at least token Roman Catholics, the women taking their faith most seriously. The second largest Christian denomination are the Anglicans. There is also a community of Seventh Day Adventists. Hindu and Muslim faiths are also represented.

Celebrating First Communion

Whom Do You Trust?

On the whole, you can trust nearly everybody. Women travelling alone should use common sense and not allow themselves to be isolated in remote corners with would-be Lotharios. Keep your valuables sensibly protected. Mugging has not yet, thank goodness, become a major feature of Seychelles life.

You should always take times arranged with Seychellois with a pinch of salt. Tour agents will be fairly reliable, but any friends/acquaintances you make will probably have a fairly loose idea of the meaning of punctuality.

Victoria taxi rank

Population

eychelles has a population of about
0,000. The majority are of African or
1alagasy origin, the descendants of slaves
r freed slaves.

This population has, over the years,
nixed extensively with those of European
– mostly French – descent. There have
lways been Indian elements amongst the
eychellois, and there is also a significant
Chinese community. Few Britons ever
ettled here.

MONEY MATTERS

Currency

The Seychelles rupee is divided into notes
of SR100, SR50, SR25 and SR10. Coins
ome in denominations of SR5, SR1, 25
ents, 10 cents and 5 cents.

Prices in shops will often be in amounts
which do not end in units of 5 or 10
cents, and unless you are paying by credit
ard, will be rounded up or down when
you are given change – usually up!

Credit Cards

Major credit cards are accepted at most
arger hotels and restaurants. Visa and
Mastercard are most commonly accepted.

Tipping

Tipping is not essential in Seychelles.
Many hotels and restaurants include a
service charge in the bill and this is accepted as sufficient.

Money Changers

Travellers' cheques, Eurocheques and
most Western currencies are accepted in
Seychelles. You will get a much better
rate of exchange from banks than hotels
or other establishments.

Saymore Bureau de Change, situated
immediately on the right as you come
through customs at the airport, offer superior exchange rates to the banks.

It is not necessary to have any Seychelles rupees before arrival as airport
banks open for all international flights.
You will get a higher rate for travellers'
cheques than for currency.

At press time, the exchange rate was
SR5.20 to US$1.

GETTING AROUND

Taxis

Taxis are plentiful on Mahé, less common
on Praslin and there is just one on La
Digue. Since there are no roads on any
other islands, there are, not surprisingly,
no taxis either. On Mahé and Praslin,
taxis are metered. The driver will nor-
mally have to be asked to switch the meter on because the system is not popular.
Do not believe drivers who claim the
price will be lower unmetered. If you call
out a taxi, tell him to switch his meter on
when he leaves to avoid any argument.
Drivers are a bit selective about the jour-
neys they are prepared to make; some are
unwilling to tackle particularly bad roads
or trips out to remote areas. Most vehicles are in good condition. If you negoti-
ate a daily or hourly rate, many of them
can be amusing, charming and informa-
tive guides to the islands.

Taxis are available at Mahé and Praslin
airports, Victoria taxi rank, Albert Street
– next door to CODEVAR Craft Centre,
and by the Clock Tower in Independence
Avenue, Victoria. They are also usually
available from larger hotels. Don't expect
to hail a taxi at any time of day or night,
especially on Praslin.

Bus

Buses are cheap and can be a good way
to get around if you have time and can
avoid the peak periods, but prepare for
long waits and a fight for seats on some

routes. Timings and routes are geared to suit the local population, not the tourist. Most routes run from about 5.30am to about 7pm, with a reduced service on Sundays and Public Holidays.

Many buses are past their prime and battle along with a tremendous clash and clatter. Some of the driving is a bit hair-raising too, especially if the bus is almost empty or it is the last run of the day. You can get thrown about a bit on the bends. The services are often unreliable because of breakdowns and limited number of vehicles available.

Car

Many car hire companies are represented at Seychelles International Airport and larger hotels. Rates are fairly standard and are for unlimited mileage. It is wise to book in advance. Cars are not always in the best of condition. Check brakes and indicators before you set off. Mini Mokes are cool and fun but the seats get wet if it rains and it is harder to secure your valuables.

Driving is on the left unlike in the US and Europe. Road signs are similar, or the same as those in Europe. One difference is, if you see what seems to be a tree

growing in the middle of the road, it means a huge pot hole has opened up and someone has considerately marked it with a branch. Speed limits are 40kph (25mph) in towns and villages, and 65kph (40mph) outside. The only exception is along Mahé's new east coast road, where the limit is 80kph (50mph).

Roads are narrow, usually with deep drainage ditches at the side. Mountain roads are steep with many very sharp bends. On Mahé, the standard of road

maintenance is high. Roads on Praslin are not so good.

Driving standards and road discipline are sloppy. Pedestrians seem oblivious to cars, especially during the weekends or public holidays when the beer has flowed a little too freely.

Victoria Service Station is open 5am–11pm daily; **Beau Vallon Service Station** 6am–9pm daily; and **Grand Anse Praslin Service Station** 7.30am–6pm Monday–Saturday, and 7.30am– noon Sunday and Public Holidays.

The Inter-Island schooner

Ferry

Schooner ferries run between the main islands of Mahé, Praslin and La Digue. The schooner *La Belle Praslinoise* takes 3 hours to cross from Praslin to Mahé while *Cousin* takes 2½ hours. *La Belle Edma* takes 3¼ hours between La Digue and Mahé. Ferries generally depart Praslin or La Digue between 5am and 6am, returning from Mahé around noon the same day. An inter-island ferry schedule can be collected from the **Tourism Division**, Ground Floor, Independence House, Independence Avenue, Victoria. Alternatively, call the ferry owner.
La Belle Praslinoise (Mr L Grandcourt), Tel: 233512
Cousin (Mr J Adrienne), Tel: 233343
La Belle Edma (Mr E Mussad), Tel: 234013

The ferry from Praslin to La Digue departs at 7am, 9.30am, 10.30am, 2.30pm and 5pm, returning at 7.30am, 10am, 11.30am, 3.30pm and 5.30pm daily, exept on Sunday and Public Holidays when the 9.30am departure and 10am return does not operate. For bookings, contact Mr W Rose (Tel: 233229 or 233859).

The ferry terminal on Mahé is the Inter-Island Quay, on Praslin the Baie Ste Anne Jetty, and on La Digue the La Passe Jetty. Do not rely on taxis being available at the other end. Telephone in advance and give the taxi driver your arrival time (see *Getting Around*).

Helicopter

There are scheduled helicopter flights to La Digue, departing from the International Airport each Friday morning and arriving 25 minutes later at L'Union, La Digue. The helicopter returns to Victoria Helistop for the day, departing again for La Digue late afternoon. A maximum of four passengers can be carried. It is often possible to turn up without booking, should you decide it's a great day to visit La Digue, but it is better to book in advance and avoid disappointment.

Transfers to Silhouette can also be arranged on Sunday mornings. These are principally for guests of Silhouette Island Lodge and bookings should be made through the **Silhouette Island Lodge** (Tel: 224003).

Transfers between certain islands and hotels may also be arranged. For these and La Digue transfers, contact **Helicopter Seychelles** (Tel: 275400).

Domestic Flights

Air Seychelles operate many flights in small planes (maximum 20 passengers), daily between Mahé and Praslin from 5.40am–6.40pm (Mahé to Praslin) and 6.05am–7.05pm (Praslin to Mahé). There is a twice-daily flight between Mahé and Frégate, daily between Mahé and Bird, four times a week between Mahé and Denis and three times a week between Desroches and Mahé.

Inter-Island planes

Mahé flights depart from the **Inter-Island Terminal**, at the north end of Seychelles International Airport. Flight time is 15 minutes to Praslin, 15 minutes to Frégate, 30 minutes to Bird or Denis and one hour to Desroches.

Special charters and photographic flights are also available. For further information contact **Air Seychelles** (Tel: 225220).

By Yacht or Motorboat

Day trips can be arranged to most islands; those further afield require boats with live aboard facilities. Details can be obtained from **Marine Charter Association** (Tel: 322126). See *Cruising* and *Fishing* under *Activities* for other contacts.

Bicycle

Unless you are a budding Olympic champion, Mahé by bike is not recommended. The roads are very steep, busy and narrow. Praslin is less busy and less mountainous. Cycles are available at Baie Ste Anne, Anse Volbert and Grand Anse. Bicycles are the way to see La Digue, where they can be hired almost everywhere, but the biggest selection is at La Passe.

HOURS & HOLIDAYS

Business Hours

Office hours are Monday–Friday 8am–4pm. Shop hours are 8.30am/9am–5/5.30pm Monday–Friday and 8.30am/9am–noon Saturday. Many shops close for lunch 12.30–1.30pm. Some shops, mainly Indian merchants outside town, are open on Saturday afternoon, Sunday and public holidays.

Public Holidays

1–2 January: New Year
March/April: Good Friday

1 May:Labour Day
18 June: National Day
Mid-June: Corpus Christi
29 June:Independence Day
15 August: Assumption
1 November: All Saints Day
8 December: Immaculate Conception
25 December: Christmas

ACCOMMODATION

Hotels

There is no official star rating system in Seychelles. Room standards are generally high but standards of service are often poor. Prices are high and you are usually better off with a package deal than paying the official rack rates. Peak season supplements may apply at Easter, Christmas/New Year and in August. It is illegal to camp or sleep rough anywhere in Seychelles.

Price categories for a double room, per night, inclusive of breakfast are:

$\quad$ *$* $\quad = \quad$ SR500 and below
$\quad$ *$$* $\quad = \quad$ SR500–SR1,000
$\quad$ *$$$* $\quad = \quad$ SR1,000–SR1,500
$\quad$ *$$$$* $\quad = \quad$ SR1,500 and above

There is no service charge or tax.

Mahé

LE MERIDIEN FISHERMAN'S COVE HOTEL
PO Box 35, Bel Ombre, Mahé
Tel: 247252
Facing Beau Vallon beach, this is a small, upmarket hotel with a club-like atmosphere. There are 48 rooms, all air-conditioned with telephone, radio, TV and en suite facilities. There are three tennis courts – two with night lighting. Guests may have a free introductory diving lesson with Seychelles Underwater Centre. *$$$$*

NORTHOLME HOTEL
PO Box 333, Glacis, Mahé
Tel: 261222
Situated over a beautiful, secluded cove, there are 12 standard and seven superior rooms with telephone, bath or shower, air-conditioning, radio and fridge. All rooms have sea views. Diving and snorkelling facilities are available and water-

sports can be arranged through a nearby hotel. This is the oldest hotel in Seychelles and it still has some of its Raffles-like ambience. Several famous authors have been guests here in the past. *$$$*

CORAL STRAND HOTEL
PO Box 400, Beau Vallon, Mahé
Tel: 247036
Situated right on Beau Vallon beach, there are 102 rooms and one suite, all air-conditioned. Mini-bars are available on request only. All rooms have telephone, radio and either a bath or shower. Hotel guests receive special rates for Leisure 2000 watersports. Guests are entitled to a free introductory diving lesson and 10 percent discount on all dives at the Seychelles Underwater Centre. Both Leisure 2000 and the Underwater Centre are within the hotel complex. *$$*

CHATEAU D'EAU
PO Box 107, Barbarons, Mahé
Tel: 378577
Opposite side of Mahé to the airport and Victoria, so it is nice and peaceful. Very pleasant location. Expensive for a guest house, but standards are high. *$$*

BLUE LAGOON CHALETS
Anse à la Mouche, Mahé
Tel: 371197
Eight self-catering chalets in a peaceful and charming location with sea views. Free windsurfing and canoeing, and arrangements can be made for diving and fishing trips. Ceiling fans with air-conditioning on request. *$$*

MOUNTAIN RISE
Sans Souci, Mahé
Tel: 225145
Tucked well away from the beach, in the cool exhilirating atmosphere of the mountains. Spectacular views. *$*

Praslin

COCO DE MER HOTEL
Anse Bois de Rose, Praslin
Tel: 233900
This is located between Grand Anse and
Baie Ste Anne on its own beautiful beach.
There are 30 spacious rooms, all with sea
views, bathroom, sitting area and bal-
cony or terrace. Each has telephone, TV,
air-conditioning and ceiling fan. Facilities include windsurfers, canoes, a tennis
court, bicycles and various games. *$$$*

INDIAN OCEAN FISHING CLUB
Grand Anse, Praslin
Tel: 233324, 233457
Situated on the beach, just five minutes
from the airport. There are 16 sea-view
rooms – with plans for eight more, all
air-conditioned with telephone and en
suite bathroom. Watersports facilities –
windsurfing, paddle skis and snorkelling
equipment – are free to residents. *$$*

LA RESERVE
Anse Petite Cour, Praslin
Tel: 232211
Situated in a beautiful, secluded cove
with excellent snorkelling. There are four
air-conditioned suites and eight villas
with ceiling fans – air-conditioning op-
tional. Suites have fax machines, all rooms
have telephones. Facilities include a tennis court, free canoeing, snorkelling gear,
sundown cruise – including drinks, and a
discovery cruise to another island with
free transport; the only cost payable is
for the barbecue. *$$*

MAISON DES PALMES
Grand Anse Praslin
Tel: 233411
On the beach, 24 bungalows with bath-
room, terrace, ceiling fans and telephone.
Watersports facilities, tennis court and
games room. Day excursions to islands
around Praslin. *$$*

CRESSWELL ART HOLIDAYS
Anse St Sauveur, Praslin
Tel: 233036
Beautiful location, right on a quiet beach.
Guests are made very much part of the
family. Friendly atmosphere and good
home cooking. Free art tuition for resi-
dents. *$*

VILLAS DE MER
Grand Anse, Praslin
Tel: 233972
Good, clean, simple facilities provided in
pleasant chalets by the sea. The cost of
breakfast is included and dinner can be
provided by arrangement if you like.

Villas De Mer's beachside chalets

Guests are given a tour of the local shops
on arrival. Snorkelling equipment available. Friendly atmosphere. *$*

HEALTH & EMERGENCIES

Hygiene/General Health

Water in tourist establishments is safe to
drink and standards of hygiene are good.

You will almost certainly be bitten by
mosquitoes, though these are only really
active around dusk. They can be discour-
aged by repellents or by lighting a mos-
quito coil – often supplied in hotel rooms.

```
         DEPARTMENT  OF  HEALTH
             LOGAN      HOSPITAL

DRESSINGS    8 AM      TO      10 AM    DAILY
             EXCEPT            EMERGENCIES
VISITING HOURS      3 PM    TO     5 PM     DAILY
CHILDREN    UNDER    10    YEARS     SHOULD
            SEEK           PERMISSION

         PLEASE        BE        QUIET

DOCTORS    CLINIC    WILL    BE    HELD    AS
FROM     MONDAY     TO      DAY   8 AM – 12 NOON
FROM     12 NOON   ONWARDS  EMERGENCY    ONLY
```

Black wasps are harmless but yellow
wasps have an extremely painful sting.
Avoid their nests which are cone-shaped
and hang from tree branches. Also, give
large centipedes a wide berth. Large millipedes are harmless.

High factor sun creams are essential.
Do not underestimate the power of the
overhead sun. Drink plenty of liquids and

not all beer or cola, which can dehydrate you. You should make a point of drinking at least a glass or two of water if you've been out on the beach all day.

The dangers of the deep for the tourist are minimal. Black sea urchins are perhaps the greatest menace. Their spines can be dissolved out of your skin by applying a little pawpaw. Cone shells have extremely painful and toxic stings. If you pick any up, even those which seem to be dead, do so by the thick end, keeping the pointed end – where the harpoon is – well away from your body. Always wear plastic shoes or other suitable footwear if you are walking over coral rock. Coral cuts can be very slow to heal. Some live corals and fish sting. If in doubt, it is far better not to touch, just look. This rule makes life better for the corals and the fish too!

Pharmacies

There are two fairly reliable pharmacies in Victoria, Mahé:
Behram's Pharmacy, Victoria Arcade, Victoria, Tel: 225559.
Fock Heng Pharmacy, Revolution Avenue, Victoria, Tel: 322751.
Lai Lam (Pty) Ltd, Market Street, Victoria, Tel: 322336.

Bring prescription medicines with you, but if you do run out, try the Dispensary at the **Out-patients Department** of Victoria Hospital. There are no pharmacies on Praslin. Go to the nearest hospital dispensary.

Medical/Dental Services

Health services are fairly good in Seychelles, although a great deal of waiting is sometimes involved, especially on a Monday morning. Larger hotels have nurses who can arrange a visit to the tourist doctor if necessary. Normal consultation hours are 8am–4pm and there is a small fee payable. There are also a limited number of private clinics.

Victoria Hospital is south of the town, next to the Botanical Gardens. There are also hospitals at Anse Royale, Mahé, on Praslin and La Digue, together with local clinics in many villages.
Useful numbers are:

Victoria Hospital, Tel: 224400.
Anse Royale Hospital, Tel: 371222.
Praslin Hospital, Tel: 233333.
La Digue Hospital, Tel: 234255.

Crime

Violent crime involving tourists is rare but casual theft is on the increase. Do not leave valuables unguarded, especially at the beach when swimming. Lock your hotel room and car. You should take the same common sense precautions you would take almost everywhere these days. The same applies to women travelling alone. Do not be fooled into thinking that because Seychelles looks like paradise, Eve's bite of the apple and its consequences do not apply here.

Police

Police uniforms are dark blue trousers or skirts, with white short-sleeved shirts or blouses, with epaulettes. Central Police Station – the headquarters – is in Revolution Avenue, Victoria. Dial 999 in an emergency; same for Fire Brigade and Ambulance.
Useful numbers are:
Central Police Station, Tel: 322011
Beau Vallon Police Station, Tel: 247242
Grand Anse (Praslin) Police Station, Tel: 233251
Baie Ste Anne Police Station, Tel: 233232
La Digue Police Station, Tel: 234251

COMMUNICATIONS AND NEWS

Post

The main post office in Victoria is open Monday–Friday 8am–4pm and Saturday 8am–noon. Most hotels and some shops sell stamps. Hotels will post mail for you. There are post boxes by police stations in the villages.

Telephone

This service is very good. Direct dialling is available to most countries. Public telephones are plentiful and **Cable & Wireless** in Victoria is open 24 hours for telephone, fax and telex services. This is worth bearing in mind as hotels generally impose a 100 percent surcharge on call costs, which are already much higher in Seychelles than elsewhere. Most public phones take only phonecards, on sale at Cable & Wireless and many shops. Some of the remoter islands have no phone service, although an increasing number are having satellite phone links installed. Costs of using these are very high.

Callers to UK who possess a BT Chargecard can dial 0800-44. A UK operator will answer and connect your call, thereby avoiding high telephone bills on your hotel account. US telephone charge cards are not yet in use here.

Useful numbers:

International Flight Enquiries, Tel: 37305

Praslin Airport, Tel: 232214

Met Office (Weather), Tel: 373377

Operator, Dial: 100

International Operator, Dial: 115

Directory Enquiries, Dial: 118

Media

There is one daily (except Sunday and Public Holidays) newspaper, the government-managed *Seychelles Nation.* Weekly newspapers include the *Regar, Seychelles Weekly* and *The Seychelles Independent.* Articles in all papers will be in three languages: English, French and Creole.

USEFUL INFORMATION

Weddings

If you can't face your in-laws to be, or all those awful relatives that have something to do with your better half, or you just want to get married in one of the world's most romantic destinations, Seychelles could be the perfect choice for you.

Assuming the whole thing is not spontaneous, then it is best to book through a tour operator, who will arrange everything from the hotel to the cake, wedding photography, live music and so on.

If it is all a bit spur of the moment, you can still make arrangements on site. We once ended up at the wedding of a rock musician who arranged a last minute surprise wedding for his girlfriend who thought she was just visiting friends for dinner. In approximately five minutes from proposal to pronouncement they were man and wife. On Mahé contact the **Registrar** (Tel: 225333) at the Civil Status Division, Independence House, Victoria, for do-it-yourself weddings. You will

need your birth certificates, passports, and if applicable, divorce papers. You need to be in Seychelles a minimum of 11 days to be eligible. If you can't be bothered to make your own arrangements, contact a reputable local travel agent.

On Praslin, we recommend you contact Verney Cresswell at **Cresswell Art Holidays** (Tel: 233036), Anse St Sauveur, who can make all the arrangements and provide the most superb location for a quietly spectacular wedding.

On Mahé, we recommend **L'Islette B** (Tel: 378229), a small island off Port Gland. This is another superb location for an unforgettable wedding.

Children

Seychelles is a fun place for children, if only because of the lovely beaches and opportunities to play in the sea. The Seychellois love children. It is one of the best ways of making friends locally. There is nothing to worry about from a health point of view, except the fierce strength of the sun. Try and get them to keep a hat on. It is quite safe to bring a babe in arms here and a mobile child who can enjoy the sea and sand but for the ages in between, it could be a wasted experience. Older children will have loads of fun with the watersports.

Maps

Detailed island maps are on sale at the **Survey Division**, Ground Floor, Independence House, Victoria.

Bookshops

There are few bookshops in Seychelles, although most gift shops will sell a range of books about Seychelles. The best bookshop is **Antigone**, Victoria Arcade, Victoria. In addition to books about Seychelles, you will also find novels in English and French. They also have kiosks at the International Airport and Inter-Island Terminal.

Other bookshops are **Oyster**, Quincy Street, Victoria, and SPACE, Huteau Lane, Victoria. European newspapers and magazines, a little out of date, can be bought at SPACE.

Photography

Film is best bought at home as it is expensive in Seychelles. Kodak and Fuji films are available here through **Photo Eden** and **Kim Koon** respectively, in Independence Avenue, Victoria, Mahé.

Most hotel shops will also sell films. Same day processing is available for both prints and slides, but it is fairly expensive and often not of top quality.

Family fun under the sun

LANGUAGE

Seychelles is trilingual: English, French and Creole are spoken. On Mahé you will have little trouble in getting by in English or French, but elsewhere a few words of Creole can help. Creole is mainly French in origin and most of the nouns will be familiar if you speak French. But the grammar is much simpler, with only one form for each verb, no sexes and no need to worry about your accent. It is written phonetically and every letter is pronounced.

English	Creole
Yes	Wi
No	Non
Hello	Bonzour
How are you?	Sava/Ki i dir?
I am well	Mon byen
Thank you	Mersi
Good afternoon	Bon apremidi
Goodbye	Orevwar
What is this?	Kisisa?
That's all	Sa menm tou
I don't understand	Mon pa konpran
Could you repeat that please?	Repete sivouple
Good	Bon
Bad	Pa bon
I don't know	Mon pa konnen
I'm hungry	Mon lafen
I'm thirsty	Mon swaf
Where is the hotel?	Kote lotel sivouple?
Where are you from?	Kote ou sorti?
I like...	Mon kontan avek...
How much does it cost?	Kombyen i vann?
That's expensive	I ser
A little bit	En ti pe
Where is the toilet?	Kote kabinen sivouple?
When?	Kan?
How?	Ki mannyer?
Why?	Akoz?
Which?	Lekel?
Shop	Laboutik
Airport	Lerpor
You	Ou
We	Nou
What?	Ki?/Kwa?
Who?	Ki?/Lekel?

Grafitti art on corrugated fence

USEFUL ADDRESSES

Tourist Information

SEYCHELLES TOURISM DIVISION
Ministry of Tourism and Transport,
Victoria, Mahé,
Seychelles
Tel: 225313
This is the only tourist office in Seychelles. They offer advice on hotels, activities etc, and some brochures, but do not provide a booking service. For bookings, it is best to go to a travel agent or direct to the facility you require.

Index

ACKNOWLEDGMENTS

Cover (T), Backcover	**Adrian Skerrett**
Cover (B)	**Christine Osborne**
Photography	**Adrian Skerrett** *and*
Pages 5B, 8/9, 13, 66, 68M, 69 (perfume), 69 (model boats), 70B, 71, 72T, 72B, 73T, 73B, 76, 77T, 81T, 90B	**Christine Osborne**
28B	**Tom Bowers**
10	**Tony Arruza**
34	**Seychelles Underwater Centre**
Senior Desktop Operator	**Suriyani Ahmad**
Handwriting	**V. Barl**
Cover Design	**Klaus Geisler**
Cartography	**Berndtson & Berndtson**